POETS OF CHILE

A BILINGUAL ANTHOLOGY 1965 -1985

Steven F. White, Editor

POETS OF CHILE
A Bilingual Anthology, 1965-1985

INTRODUCTION BY JUAN ARMANDO EPPLE

GREENSBORO: UNICORN PRESS   1986

The painting by Roberto Arroyo is reproduced by permission.
All rights reserved by Unicorn Press.
The translator was aided in his work in Chile by a Fulbright grant.
Grateful acknowledgement is made by Unicorn Press to the following poets, publishers and literary executors to reprint the poems in this volume in their original language:

RAÚL ZURITA with the permission of Editorial Universitaria, S.A., Santiago, Chile *(Purgatorio)*, copyright 1979 and Editores Asociados Ltda., Santiago, Chile *(Anteparaíso)*, copyright 1982;

RODRIGO LIRA with permission of the poet's parents, Gabriel Lira and his wife, Elisa, literary executors;

ARMANDO RUBIO with permission of the poet's father, Alberto Rubio, literary executor;

Personal permission has been given by the following poets by whom all rights are reserved: OSCAR HAHN, OMAR LARA, JUAN LUIS MARTÍNEZ, JAIME QUEZADA, MANUEL SILVA ACEVEDO, WALDO ROJAS, WALTER HOEFLER, PAZ MOLINA, GONZALO MILLÁN, JUAN CAMERON, DIEGO MAQUIEIRA, CLEMENTE RIEDEMANN, TERESA CALDERÓN, ARISTÓTELES ESPAÑA, GONZALO MUÑOZ, SERGIO MANSILLA, and MAURICIO ELECTORAT.

Teo Savory, editor-in-chief of Unicorn Press, wishes to thank Anita Richardson of Universal Printing, Greensboro, North Carolina, for typesetting this book (in 11 pt Baskerville) and Inter Collegiate Press, Shawnee Mission, Kansas, for printing it (on a 70# acid-free sheet); *designed by Alan Brilliant*. Sarah Lindsay copy-edited and proof-read *Poets of Chile*, which was clothbound in the studios of Unicorn Press.

The translator wishes to thank the editors of the following magazines in which some of the poems in this anthology first appeared:
ANOTHER CHICAGO MAGAZINE, BLAKETIMES, CENTRAL PARK, GREEN-FIELD REVIEW, LATIN AMERICAN PERSPECTIVE (Sage Publications), MUNDUS ARTIUM, THE POETRY REVIEW, PRICKLY PEAR (Tucson), REVIEW (Center for Inter-American Relations), SILVERFISH REVIEW, STAND, THIRD RAIL, and WILLOW SPRINGS MAGAZINE.

Library of Congress Cataloguing in Publication Data:
```
Poets of Chile.

    Poems in Spanish; with English translations by
S.F. White.
    Bibliography: p.
    1. Chilean poetry--20th century--Translations into
English.  2. English poetry--Translations from
Spanish.  3. Chilean poetry--20th century.  I. White,
Steven F., 1955-
PQ8063.E5P64  1986        861        85-16479
ISBN 0-87775-179-X
ISBN 0-87775-180-3 (pbk.)
```
Unicorn Press Inc.
Post Office Box 3307
Greensboro, NC 27402

FOR MY FRIENDS IN CHILE

whose tenacity is an ongoing source of inspiration

En medio de la noche me pregunto,
qué pasará con Chile?
Qué será de mi pobre pobre patria oscura?

Pablo Neruda

Table of Contents

Introduction

NEW TERRITORIES OF CHILEAN POETRY

Chile is a country with an international reputation for the quality and originality of its poets: Vicente Huidobro, Gabriela Mistral (1945 Nobel Prize) and Pablo Neruda (1971 Nobel Prize), among others. A cultural tradition more formidable than that of many other countries makes it very difficult for a poet to gain recognition. Young writers must not only absorb this legacy of poetry, but also seek their own styles of expression which will renew form and language. This, of course, is a phenomenon that occurs everywhere. But poets in Chile, generation after generation, have consistently maintained high literary standards. Consequently, the competition among newcomers is very rigorous.

This anthology explores the various topographies that define the map of new Chilean poetry: a poetry in movement, in the process of formulating a language for the circumstances, challenges and dreams of Chile's collective history during the last two decades. Themes of the poetry included here treat a wide variety of subjective, social and cultural experiences in a search for new ways to represent the world through the written word. *Poets of Chile: 1965-1985* is a way of showing that Chile, an integral part of Hispanic America's cultural panorama, continues to be a space conquered by poetry.

"New Chilean poetry" is a phrase used in Chile as a means of creating generations and came into the country's literary life around 1965. By coincidence, it is a date that lies between the triumph of the Cuban Revolution (which awoke a new social/cultural awareness throughout the continent) and the electoral victory of Salvador Allende in Chile (an innovative and optimistic time of changes in Chilean history).

In 1965, the literary group *Trilce*, which was founded the year before by Omar Lara and other young poets in the southern city of Valdivia, organized the First Meeting of Young Chilean Poets. This gathering attempted a critical evaluation of the literary contribution of the previous generation of writers who began to publish in the 1950s: Miguel Arteche,

Efraín Barquero, Enrique Lihn, David Rosenmann, Alberto Rubio, Jorge Teillier and Armando Uribe Arce. It was characterized by dialogue between these authors and an innovative sector of literary critics composed of university professors. The result of this experiment was published in *Poesía chilena, 1960-1965* (Santiago: Editorial Universitaria, 1966), edited by Omar Lara and Carlos Cortínez.

In 1967, *Trilce* convoked the second national meeting of poetry, this time to highlight the work of those poets who were a part of a new generation: Walter Hoefler, Omar Lara, Gonzalo Millán, Jaime Quezada, Waldo Rojas and Manuel Silva Acevedo.* The goals of the meeting included measuring this new work in terms of the poetry in Chile that preceded it and coming to some kind of conclusion as to the new poetry's possible affiliations, influences and differences. To achieve this, the organizers proposed that each poet read a selection of his work and present a text that formulated his poetic *credo*. This last requirement was avoided by the majority of the poets, who limited themselves to a reading of their poems and thereby implicitly demonstrated their belief that poetics ought to be contained in the poem itself as a self-sufficient manifesto.

Two concerns became the generational point of departure of these young poets. On the one hand, they wanted to assess the heritage of Chilean poetry in light of their conviction that literature is a cultural manifestation that evolves historically and creates the possibility for future voices to define the world's unknown experiences more fully. As attentive readers, they sensed that a country's poetry renovates insofar as it assimilates the tradition on which it is based and then proceeds to creatively modify its horizons. On the other hand, there was the desire to reactivate literary events by establishing links and work projects between diverse groups of poets organized simultaneously in different cities. These groups sought the support (but not the tutelage) of certain universities: *Trilce* in Valdivia; Arúspice in Concepción; *Tebaida* in Arica; the writers workshops at the Catholic University and the University of Chile in Santiago, etc. By means of this relationship, the young poets hoped to generate and explore the new poetic roads that help give meaning to the present.

The social and cultural climate of the country in the mid-1960s was characterized by an increased concern to analyze and discuss basic aspects of Chilean society that needed to be changed. This activity existed in all areas of national life, including the literary work of the young writers. In opposition to the individualistic, sometimes solitary, conception, a group awareness predominated in which the meetings, readings and publications of magazines were more important than the search for personal success and individual recognition.

---

*Other participants not in this anthology included Carlos Cortínez, Ronald Kay, Luis A. Faúndez, Hernán Lavín Cerda, Floridor Pérez, Federico Schopf, and Enrique Valdés.

In 1972, the Third National Meeting of Young Poets was organized. Under the Popular Unity government, there was a complex and rich process of social transformation and, naturally, the young poets felt the need to clarify their form of participation in this new stage of Chilean history. At this meeting there was a public declaration supporting the important efforts for social change led by President Salvador Allende. But no programmatic line was set forth as to what the new culture ought to be, nor were any literary "manifestos" presented. Despite the determination and the temptation to propose absolute truths, what prevailed was the feeling of living in a time that would be clarified only in the act of living it.

The young poets, aware that they were on the threshold of a new reality that demanded a personal commitment as well as a different language, were faced with a dilemma. They resolved the problem in a way that appears to be contradictory but which, in truth, is deeply coherent. Almost all the writers incorporated themselves in Chile's process of social change, generally concentrating their activities in the field of culture. But they also saw themselves as inheritors of a poetic tradition that had, in different ways, explored and resolved the problems of the relation between language and reality. For this reason, they avoided the allure of writing a politicized poetry that would define the social sentiments of the people. They opted for an introspective poetry that was based on individual experience in order to clarify the relation between the self and the everyday life that evolves historically.

This is quite different from what occurred with the "Chilean New Song" movement which rapidly became a powerful channel for the dissemination of the social aspirations of a large part of the Chilean people. Literary criticism has not recognized the fact that the so-called social or political poetry can be found, with greater legitimacy, in this artistic expression designed for mass audiences.

The voices that had dominated the panorama of Chilean poetry since the beginning of the 1960s, with which younger writers had to come to terms, were those of Nicanor Parra, Enrique Lihn and Jorge Teillier*. These three poets maintain a certain skepticism that distances them from the founding projects of the great poets Huidobro, De Rokha and Neruda. Parra, Lihn and Teillier chose to delve deeper into the contradictions of the present. Their position was one that doubted the ways that the world had been represented by the preceding poets and even the effectiveness of the poet as spokesperson of a decisive truth. These new forms of expression soon achieved the rank of literary models.

---

*This is not to forget the legendary presence of Neruda, a poet who rewrote and expanded his monumental cycles of poetry in a process that goes far beyond his physical death.

Nicanor Parra's book, *Poemas y antipoemas* (1954)*, revolutionized the conception of the lyrical speaker and poetic language. In his anti-poetry, the speaker ceases to be that infallible figure, the "small God" postulated by Huidobro that offered absolute truths. In Parra's poetry, the protagonist is transformed into the common man who lives the contradictory life of the modern city, who loves and hates, who makes mistakes, and who communicates his anti-heroic experience in a colloquial language.

Enrique Lihn, beginning with his book, *La pieza oscura* (1963)**, develops a poetry which moves between the speaker's distrust of language's capacity to faultlessly define reality and the conviction that, nevertheless, the act of writing is the only means the poet possesses of saving himself from conformity or absolute isolation. Lihn retreats into the reality of writing itself and questions the activity of creating poetry. In this way he succeeds in constructing a poetic universe of multiple associations that explores with irony and compassion the deep contradictions of the contemporary poet and humanity in general.

Jorge Teillier, whose work unfortunately has not been translated into English, represents a tendency in Chilean poetry known as *poesía lárica*. This term could be translated as poetry of the ancestral land, or poetry that recounts the lost paradise of childhood and investigates the primordial origins of man.

Teillier's two key books, *Muertes y maravillas* (an anthology of poems published between 1953 and 1970) and *Para un pueblo fantasma* (1978), describe the opposition that exists between a fragile historic present and the "secret reality" that remains hidden with brilliant flashes in the everyday spaces of the common man—the kind of person who will never appear in the pages of newspapers or on television. The poet searches beyond what's ephemeral and illusory in modern society and tries to find an ancestral order that survives with its secret symbols in forgotten rural villages not yet destroyed by urbanization and technology. This metaphysical return to the magic world of childhood and to the harmonious order of a rural space closer to the cosmic cycle of Nature's deaths and regenerations does not imply a rejection of history and its requirements for change. Rather, it is a search for those natural bases of life that are often forgotten in the contingencies of historical developments that man must confront. Teillier's poetry defines a double road of vital apprenticeship. The lyric speaker repeatedly describes the intimate experience of his travels between the rural village and the capital by utilizing the motif of the journey by train where he writes many of his poems. At the same time, he also evokes the figures and the poetic language of writers such as Villon,

---

*Two collections of Parra's poetry, *Poems and Anti-poems* and *Emergency Poems*, have been published by New Directions.
**New Directions also published an anthology of Lihn's poetry: *The Dark Room & Other Poems*.

Fournier, and René-Guy Cadou, who in their times spoke of the historical changes in France. In this way, Teillier (of French descent) can read their works in the context of Chile's evolving history.

The young poets who began to publish in the mid-1960s assimilated these poetic tendencies but did not adhere to them as obligatory models. They had their own diverse thematic and stylistic concerns. Before seeking to establish a point of departure radically different from what preceded them, the young poets wanted to learn from it based on as unbiased a view as possible of literature as reality. The following voices represent part of a generation formed in a period of solid cultural apprenticeship: Omar Lara's poetry rooted in the subjective experience of the passage of time and the links of love; the densely self-reflexive poetry whose referent is the disquieting and elusive "art of the word" by Waldo Rojas; the baroque discourse by Oscar Hahn that recreates and modernizes the motifs and expressive forms of certain poetry from the Spanish Golden Age; the objectivism of the poetry by Gonzalo Millán in which the visual perception of life (and the objects that an industrial society uses) creates a distance that forces the reader to re-examine the relationship between man and the surrounding world; the epigrammatic precision of Walter Hoefler's poems; and the enumerative qualities of the open poems by Manuel Silva Acevedo.

The military coup of 1973 meant not only a violent rupture in the country's social and political life, but also an interruption in the cultural process which had been characterized until that time by an open dialogue with the land, the history and the traditions of Chile. A significant number of Chilean intellectuals, writers and artists were forced into exile and had to re-orient their work in keeping with the experiences of life and the possibilities of communication with different foreign cultures. Those who remained in Chile, under a regime that imposed censorship on all cultural manifestations that made reference to the social dimension of life and its problems, created a system of self-defense known as self-censorship. These poets were obliged to retreat to private circles of creation. They had to struggle, at great risk, in order to gradually reconquer a public space for a national culture which has currently evolved into a dissident culture.

The generation that emerged during the decade before the coup suddenly became the disparate generation. But the precarious condition of its members as travelers without a round-trip ticket did not silence the voices of poetry. Paradoxically, it has given the poets an increased sense of self-confidence. The majority of these writers renewed their literary work by publishing books that include the most important poems from their prior production in a kind of self-evaluation that shows their faith in the legitimacy of the poetry they were writing before the coup. These "anthologies" also include poems written in exile. The poets simultaneously re-evaluated their distant country's historical and cultural identity and opened themselves to other countries and cultures.

In Chile, it was thought for some years that the "cultural blackout" provoked by the coercive measures of the dictatorship's official apparatus had blocked all possibilities of free artistic activities. Between 1973 and 1976, the country went through a phase of disarticulation of its historic means of existence and of its national identity. The Pinochet government tried to impose a free market economic system and at the same time to control the circulation of ideas by permitting only those that expressed individualistic values. But between 1976 and 1981 (the boom years of the economic model and the period in which certain contradictions in the regime's ideological orientation appeared) a new generation of poets began to create a public aperture under extremely difficult circumstances. Many of these writers had to educate themselves despite the fact that they were cut off from Chile's past and from the previous generation which was forced into exile almost in its entirety. In a world of incommunication, poetry renewed its secret and overt mission of clarifying the new situations of life and breaking through isolation and solitude. These new poems circulated not in books, but in makeshift magazines, small literary groups and poetic gatherings and, above all, in readings associated with other public acts.

Because the alternatives for disseminating the work were limited to "listening" situations at universities, cafes and certain public places, the prevailing tone of the poetry is narrative and appeals directly to the audience on an emotional level, thereby allowing the public to share the critiques and hopes of the poet. Some of the recourses of this poetry are irony, humor and subtle double meanings that often require the complicity of the reader or the listener who must understand not only what is said but also what is left implicit. The poets' attitudes are based on means of expression that range from the old chronicles to television commercials. They allude to the complexity of a reality that cannot be adequately interpreted by a single voice. In the current historical context of Chile, many new poets have redefined in this way the function of poetry and the value of the word as a vehicle of communication.

, Two young poets who had begun their literary labor before the coup in a loosely knit group of writers that met at the Café Cinema in Viña del Mar started to define a radically new space of meanings by the mid-1970s. Their work revolved around the contradiction between the logic of language and reality's lack of logic.

The poetry of Juan Luis Martínez explores the frontiers between the intuition and the rationality of inherited forms of communication. It also investigates the tension that exists between fictionalized reality in logical discourse and the poetic fiction that becomes real. His poems consist of axioms that mutually nullify each other with a logic of the absurd that refers, perhaps out of opposition, to the apparent logic of the real world. Martínez's poetry undoes the limits of poetry as a genre and, at the same time, raises doubts concerning man's cognitive abilities.

Raúl Zurita, who is certainly the most well-known poet in the generation emerging today in Chile, is developing an ambitious poetry project that consists of three books representing clearly delineated stages in a process of rebirth. It is a reformulation of Chile's intimate and collective identity. Zurita's poetry has the best characteristics of a vanguardistic art. The poet, a figure torn apart by the pain, anguish and lack of meaning in the world, proposes to reconstruct heaven on earth—from the edge of the void where he passes. It is a proposition (in the literal and metaphorical sense) to create a new map of the country, a new human territory. His voice, both subjective and prophetic, rediscovers the natural space needed in order to establish a utopia. This dream of the future is, for the moment, a weaving together of words in constant and disquieting movement.

Other poets included in this anthology offer a different way of reading the past and of defining history and national myths—for example Diego Maquieira's treatment of the popular festival called *La Tirana* and Sergio Mansilla's use of mythology from the island of Chiloé. Clemente Riedemann rescues the language of the chroniclers (perhaps as an act of ideological subversion of that literary language) and seeks to formulate the triple legacy that has shaped the history of southern Chile: the indigenous population, the Spaniards, and the Germans. In other cases, the poets* begin to define the world based on the concrete and contradictory circumstances of the present in an attempt to redeem a humanity that has been violently abused by the events of its times.

The case of Aristóteles España is exceptional in that the poet assumes the dangerous task (in the social and the literary sense) of writing testimonial poetry—a form of expression generally reserved in Chile for the short story or the novel. España succeeds in resolving, with literary rigor, the distance that often exists in all testimony between the factual recounting of the experience and the creation of an aesthetic sense for that experience. In some of the poems, however, there is sometimes a hiatus that is too great between the immediacy of what was endured and the dream of the future

---

*including Juan Cameron, Paz Molina, Aristóteles España, Teresa Calderón, Mauricio Electorat and Rodrigo Lira

that guides the protagonist. This distance between the present and the future, transformed into literary difficulty, also represents for the reader the real problems of collective change in Chilean society over the last twenty years.

Finally, it is clear that in several young poets' works there is an attempt not only to modify the language of poetry by amplifying the genre's parameters to include languages taken from other arts, but also to incorporate attitudes, situations and problems previously absent from the horizons of national concerns—feminism, ecology and alternate lifestyles that reflect a changing, multifaceted society.

Thus, Chilean poets, in another moment of their evolution, renew the commitment that no one has asked of them but that, nevertheless, they persist in fulfilling: reformulating the changing human and historic geography of the country in which they live. And this is a territory founded with new words.

Juan Armando Epple

UNIVERSITY OF OREGON

TRANSLATOR'S PREFACE

My attempt to begin this project in 1978 was cut short by an illness which caused many friends to remember me as *el hepatítico* when I returned to Chile nearly five years later to finish my work. The interim between visits had created significant, although relative, changes in the level of cultural activities in the capital as well as in the provinces—more books, more readings, more forums. But, while 1983 was a year of great hope in Chile, it was also one of great violence.

When the sea is too rough for fishing, the fishermen on the island of Chiloé in southern Chile *hacen quercún*. They paint their boats, repair nets and keep busy, sometimes working together and other times alone, until the storm passes. This is a good metaphor for the attitude of many Chilean poets I met both inside and outside Chile during the elaboration of this anthology—a sampling of poetry produced over the last twenty years. These are difficult historical waters for the poet and the anthologist to navigate.

The selection of writers in this book is a partial representation of the two most recent generations of Chilean poets with as much diversity as possible. By means of a bilingual format, I have tried to create a bridge of words between North and South America. Interestingly enough, the book is, at the same time, a way of joining the work of two generations unfamiliar with each other's literary production as a result of the military coup in 1973 which severed the generational dialogue.

It may be true, as one Chilean poet told me, that one can lift any stone in Chile and find a poet. In my travels from Arica in the north to Punta Arenas in the south (roughly equivalent to the distance between Portland, Oregon and Portland, Maine), I found that there was certainly no shortage of poets. The problem was making the hard choices that define an anthology's bias.

Standards of excellence in Chile are high when it comes to poetry. But work by these and other younger poets will undoubtedly continue to renew the country's rich poetic heritage. Perhaps these versions in English, despite the unplanned but inevitable obsolescence of any translation, will help bring some of this constantly evolving tradition to readers in the United States who have already shown their receptivity to Hispanic American literature.

Steven F. White

OSCAR HAHN

(1938)

The division of writers into generations is often an arbitrary task undertaken by critics to give order to a literary panorama that rejects such boundaries. While Oscar Hahn, for example, is only three years younger than Jorge Teillier, the two poets are associated with different generations. In this case, the criteria seem to be publications. In 1961 when Hahn published his first book, Teillier, in keeping with the Chilean tradition of precociousness, had published three. Hahn has always maintained a slow pace of poetic production. Until 1981, his work consisted of 42 gem-like texts joined in a single self-anthology—*Arte de morir* (Art of Dying). His most recent book, *Imágenes nucleares* (Nuclear Images), is another anthology of six previously published poems that take on an entirely different character in their new context. During a presentation of this book in Santiago, the Chilean poet, Enrique Lihn, commented on the fact that the first important poem in Hahn's work, 'The Reincarnation of the Butchers,' was written at the age of 17 to commemorate the tenth anniversary of the bombing of Hiroshima. Lihn went on to hypothesize that perhaps, in a symbolic way, the atomic explosion gave birth to a poet. In this sense, Hahn is a Nuclear Age descendent of the Huidobro who wrote the apocalyptic poem, "Ecuatorial," during World War I. Hahn's poetry is a combination of formal elements derived from poetry of Spain's Golden Age and contemporary everyday Chilean Spanish. Hahn is from the northern port city of Iquique and taught in Arica until September of 1973. He currently teaches Hispanic American literature at the University of Iowa. Although he has lived in the United States for a decade, Hahn visits Chile frequently and continues to be an important part of literary activities there.

REENCARNACIÓN DE LOS CARNICEROS

Y salió otro caballo, rojo: y al que
estaba sentado sobre éste, le fue dado
quitar de la tierra la paz, y hacer que
los hombres se matasen unos a otros.

San Juan, *Apocalipsis*

Y vi que los carniceros al tercer día,
al tercer día de la tercera noche,
comenzaban a florecer en los cementerios
como brumosos lirios o como líquenes.

Y vi que los carniceros al tercer día,
llenos de tordos que eran ellos mismos,
volaban persiguiéndose, persiguiéndose,
constelados de azufres fosforescentes.

Y vi que los carniceros al tercer día,
rojos como una sangre avergonzada,
jugaban con siete dados hechos de fuego
pétreos como los dientes del silencio.

Y vi que los perdedores al tercer día,
se reencarnaban en toros, cerdos o carneros
y vegetaban como animales en la tierra
para ser carne de las carnicerías.

Y vi que los carniceros al tercer día,
se están matando entre ellos perpetuamente.
Tened cuidado, señores los carniceros,
con los terceros días de las terceras noches.

REINCARNATION OF THE BUTCHERS

> And there went out another horse that
> was red: and power was given to him
> that sat thereon to take peace from the
> earth, and that they should kill one
> another.
>
> Revelation 6: 4

And on the third day I saw the butchers,
the third day of the third night,
as they blossomed in the cemeteries
like lilies the color of fog or lichens.

And on the third day I saw the butchers,
filled with the crying crows they were,
flying in pursuit of each other,
shining like stars of phosphorescent sulphur.

And on the third day I saw the butchers,
redder than the blood of shame,
playing with the seven dice made of fire
and the stone teeth of silence.

And on the third day I saw the losers
reincarnated as bulls, pigs or lambs,
grazing the face of the earth
to be meat in the butcher shops.

And on the third day I saw the butchers
slaughtering each other until the end of time.
You! Butchers! Beware
of the third days of the third nights!

OSCAR HAHN

CIUDAD EN LLAMAS

Entrando en la ciudad por alta mar
la grande bestia vi su rojo ser
Entré por alta luz por alto amor
entréme y encontréme padecer
Un sol al rojo blanco en mi interior
crecía y no crecía sin cesar
y el alma con las hordas del calor
templóse y contemplóse crepitar
Ardiendo el más secreto alrededor
mi cuerpo en llamas vivas vi flotar
y en medio del silencio y del dolor
hundióse y confundióse con la sal:
entrando en la ciudad por alto amor
entrando en la ciudad por alta mar

CITY ON FIRE

A great sea carried me
to the city.
I saw the huge beast,
its red core.
I entered on great light,
on great love.
Fear rose and grew
without growing,
kept rising.
A white-hot sun
inside me. And my soul,
teeming with heat,
waited in peace to watch
itself burn.
The last secrets crackled.
I saw the living flames
and my body floating
in silence, pain.
It sank and dissolved in salt.
A great sea carried me
to the city.
Love.

VISIÓN DE HIROSHIMA

> arrojó sobre la triple ciudad un
> proyectil único, cargado con la
> potencia del universo.
>
> Mamsala Purva
> Texto sánscrito milenario

Ojo con el ojo numeroso de la bomba,
que se desata bajo el hongo vivo.
Con el fulgor del Hombre no vidente, ojo y ojo.
Los ancianos huían decapitados por el fuego,
encallaban los ángeles en cuernos sulfúricos
decapitados por el fuego,
se varaban las vírgenes de aureola radiactiva
decapitadas por el fuego.
Todos los niños emigraban decapitados por el cielo.
No el ojo manco, no la piel tullida, no sangre
sobre la calle derretida vimos:
los amantes sorprendidos en la cópula,
petrificados por el magnésium del infierno,
los amantes inmóviles en la vía pública,
y la mujer de Lot
convertida en columna de uranio.
El hospital caliente se va por los desagües,
se va por las letrinas tu corazón helado,
se van a gatas por debajo de las camas,
se van a gatas verdes e incendiadas
que maúllan cenizas.
La vibración de las aguas hace blanquear al cuervo
y ya no puedes olvidar esa piel adherida a los muros
porque derrumbamiento beberás, leche en escombros.
Vimos las cúpulas fosforecer, los ríos
anaranjados pastar, los puentes preñados
parir en medio del silencio.
El color estridente desgarraba
el corazón de sus propios objetos:
el rojo sangre, el rosado leucemia,
el lacre llaga, enloquecidos por la fisión.

VISION OF HIROSHIMA

Keep your eyes peeled for the numerous eye of the bomb
unleashed beneath the living mushroom.
Keep your eyes peeled
for the brilliance of what Man did not foresee.
Old people fleeing decapitated by fire,
angels running aground on sulphur horns
decapitated by fire.
All the headless children migrating in the sky.
Not merely the maimed eye, the crippled skin
or blood shed in the streets. We saw:
couples surprised as they made love,
petrified by the magnesium hell,
rigid lovers in public streets
and Lot's wife
turned into a column of uranium,
hospitals boiling down drains and
your frozen heart flowing into sewers,
crawling under beds
green and burning
and howling ash.
The vibration of the waters
makes the crow turn white.
And you can't forget the skin
clinging to the walls
because you will drink ruin,
milk in the rubble.
We saw the steeples glow, the orange
rivers graze, the pregnant bridges
give birth in silence.
Screeching colors seized
what belonged to the heart:
blood red, leukemia pink,
wounded crimson,
everything driven insane by fission.

El aceite nos arrancaba los dedos de los pies,
las sillas golpeaban las ventanas
flotando en marejadas de ojos,
los edificios licuados se veían chorrear
por troncos de árboles sin cabeza,
y entre las vías lácteas y las cáscaras,
soles o cerdos luminosos
chapotear en las charcas celestes.

Por los peldaños radiactivos suben los pasos,
suben los peces quebrados por el aire fúnebre.
¿Y qué haremos con tanta ceniza?

Oil ripped toes from feet,
chairs smashed through windows
and sailed on building waves of eyes,
liquid skyscrapers dripped
from headless treetrunks
and among milky ways and fruit peels
we saw suns or luminous hogs
wallowing in celestial pools.

Something climbs a radioactive stairway.
Broken fish rise in the funereal air.
And what will we do with so much ash?

FOTOGRAFÍA

alguien desarrollaba
el negativo de su existencia.
Braulio Arenas

En la pieza contigua,
alguien revela el negativo de tu muerte.
El ácido penetra por el ojo de la cerradura.
De la pieza contigua, alguien entra en tu pieza.
Ya no estás en el lecho:
desde la foto húmeda miras tu cuerpo inmóvil.
Alguien cierra la puerta.

LA MUERTE ESTÁ SENTADA
A LOS PIES DE MI CAMA

Mi cama está deshecha: sábanas en el suelo
y frazadas dispuestas a levantar el vuelo.
La muerte dice ahora que me va a hacer la cama.
Le suplico que no, que la deje deshecha.
Ella insiste y replica que esta noche es la fecha.
Se acomoda y agrega que esta noche me ama.
Le contesto que cómo voy a ponerle cuernos
a la vida. Contesta que me vaya al infierno.
La muerte está sentada a los pies de mi cama.
Esta muerte empeñosa se calentó conmigo
y quisiera dejarme más chupado que un higo.
Yo trato de espantarla con una enorme rama.
Ahora dice que quiere acostarse a mi lado
sólo para dormir, que no tenga cuidado.
Por respeto me callo que sé su mala fama.
La muerte está sentada a los pies de mi cama.

PHOTOGRAPH

> . . . Someone was developing
> the negative of his existence.
>
> Braulio Arenas

In the room next door,
someone develops the negative of your death.
The acid penetrates through the keyhole.
From the room next door, someone enters your room.
And you're no longer in bed:
from the damp photograph you watch your stiff body.
Someone shuts the door.

DEATH IS SITTING
AT THE FOOT OF MY BED

My bed isn't made: sheets on the floor
and blankets rumpled like birds about to fly.
Death tells me that she's going to make the bed now.
I tell her not to, I beg her to leave it alone.
She insists and replies that tonight is the night.
She makes herself at home and adds that tonight she'll love me.
I ask her how I'm going to cheat on life.
She tells me to go to hell.
Death is sitting at the foot of my bed.
This persistent death wanted to get it on with me.
She wanted to leave me sucked cleaner than a fig.
I try to frighten her with an enormous branch.
She says she wants to come to bed with me—
just to sleep. She tells me not to worry.
Out of respect, I keep quiet, because I know her reputation.
Death is sitting at the foot of my bed.

PEQUEÑOS FANTASMAS

Nuestros hijos amor mío
son pequeños fantasmas

Los escucho reírse en el jardín
Los siento jugar en el cuarto vacío

Y si alguien golpea la puerta
corren a esconderse debajo de mi sábana

los pequeños fantasmas
los hijos que nunca tuvimos
y los que nunca tendremos

EL CENTRO DEL DORMITORIO

Un ojo choca contra las torres del sueño
y se queja por cada uno de sus fragmentos
mientras cae la nieve en las calles de Iowa City
la triste nieve la sucia nieve de hogaño

Algo nos despertó en medio de la noche
quizá un pequeño salto un pequeño murmullo
posiblemente los pasos de una sombra en el césped
algo difícil de precisar pero flotante

Y aquello estaba allí: de pie en el centro del dormitorio
con una vela sobre la cabeza
y la cera rodándole por las mejillas

Ahora me levanto ahora voy al baño ahora tomo agua
ahora me miro en el espejo: y desde el fondo
eso también nos mira
con su cara tan triste con sus ojos llenos de cera
mientras cae la nieve en el centro del dormitorio
la triste nieve la sucia nieve de hogaño

LITTLE GHOSTS

Our children, my love
are little ghosts

I hear them laughing in the garden
I listen to them playing in the empty room

And if someone knocks on the door
they run and hide beneath my sheet

the little ghosts
the children we never had
and those we'll never have

IN THE CENTER OF THE BEDROOM

An eye crashes into the towers of the dream
and cries for each one of its fragments
while the snow covers the streets of Iowa City
the sad snow the dirty snows of nowadays

Something woke us in the middle of the night
perhaps some small thud or some whispering
possibly the footsteps of a shadow on the lawn
something hard to describe but floating

And then it was there—standing in the center of the bedroom
with a candle on top of its head
and the wax rolling down its cheeks

Now I get up now I go to the bathroom now I drink water
now I look at myself in the mirror: and in the background
it's looking at us, too,
with such a sad face and eyes filled with wax
while the snow falls in the center of the bedroom
the sad snow the dirty snows of nowadays

TELEVIDENTE

Aquí estoy otra vez de vuelta
en mi cuarto de Iowa City

Tomo a sorbos mi plato de sopa Campbell
frente al televisor apagado

La pantalla refleja la imagen
de la cuchara entrando en mi boca

Y soy el aviso comercial de mí mísmo
que anuncia nada a nadie

HOTEL DE LAS NOSTALGIAS

Música de Elvis Presley (Q. E. P. D.)

Nosotros
    los adolescentes de los años 50
    los del jopo en la frente y el pucho en la comisura
    los bailarines de rock and roll al compás del reloj
    los jóvenes coléricos maníacos discomaníacos

dónde estamos ahora
que la vida es de minutos nada más
en qué campo de concentración

    asilados en qué embajada
    en qué país desterrados
    enterrados
    en qué cementerio clandestino

Porque no somos nada sino perros sabuesos
Nada sino perros

WATCHING T.V.

Here I am again
back in my room in Iowa City

I sip my bowl of Campbell's soup
in front of the television that isn't on

The screen reflects the image
of the spoon entering my mouth

I'm the commercial of myself
announcing nothing to no one

HEARTBREAK HOTEL

Music of Elvis Presley (R.I.P.)

We
    were the kids of the fifties
    the ones with pompadours
    and cigs in the corners of our mouths
    rock, rock, rock around the clock
    angry kids   maniacs   discomaniacs

where are we now?
life is just minutes long
in what concentration camp

            refugees in what embassy
            exiled in what country
            buried
            in what clandestine cemetery

    Because we ain't nothin' but hound
dogs
Nothing but dogs

OMAR LARA

(1941)

In April of 1965, Omar Lara, founder of the literary magazine *Trilce*, convened a National Meeting of Young Chilean Poets which he helped organize. In his statement, he hoped that the three day encounter in Valdivia would "leave a simple burning trail of the poetic word." The gathering marked a generational juncture in Chilean poetry. The younger poets invited their predecessors of the Generation of 1950 and it became clear in the ensuing dialogue that the new writers would be recipients rather than iconoclasts. All of this cultural exchange ended abruptly, however, in September of 1973 when the so-called Generation of 1965 was transformed into The Decimated Generation. The experience of many of these writers has been one of jail, repression, exile, self-censorship and clandestine lives.

Omar Lara left Chile with many of his generational compatriots. His book, *Oh buenas maneras*, which contains poems written during his imprisonment in Valdivia, won a Casa de las Américas prize in 1975. Lara's poetry is often autobiographical and anecdotal in its themes as well as discursive and colloquial in its tone. The personal history of the poet converted into poetry reflects a truncated historical project and the tragic consequences of a fascist military coup. Lara recently left Spain, after receiving a Guggenheim grant, to return to Chile.

FOTOGRAFÍA

Ese de la derecha, en cuclillas, debajo de la barbita de Lenin,
ese soy yo.
Es en una ciudad que vi y no vi,
tal vez estuve en ella, esta fotografía me inquieta,
debo averiguar hasta qué punto yo soy en esa imagen.
Anduve dando tumbos en esa ciudad.
Despertaba en la noche y me encontraba en ella,
con esfuerzo volvía a la realidad. Incluso tuve amores
con una muchacha, hasta que me confesó
ser sólo un espejismo. Desde entonces
evito salir sin un plano, ahora último repleto mis bolsillos
con pastillas de variado uso
y de vez en cuando me inclino sobre el pasto y huelo,
porque reconozco, de veras, el olor de las calles que conozco,
y distingo debajo de la lluvia, por el sabor del barro
el lugar donde estoy.

PAISAJE

a Luis Bustamante

Sorpresivamente el cielo se puso de un color
*   anaranjado*
y en las nubes se formaron espacios como grietas
con un fondo azul intenso.
Más tarde todo pareció arder
y sobre los cerros negros hasta entonces invisibles
vimos caer una ceniza roja.

PHOTOGRAPH

The one on the right, crouching down, under Lenin's goatee—
that's me.
It's in a city I saw and didn't see.
Perhaps I was there. This photograph bothers me.
I should figure out how much of me is in that image.
I wandered and stumbled through that city.
I woke up at night and found myself there.
It took a lot of effort to return to reality.
I had an affair with a girl until she admitted
she was only a mirage. Ever since then
I try not to go out without a map, lately
I've been filling my pockets with pills of different kinds
and sometimes I stretch out in the grass and
take a deep breath, because I recognize the smell
of the streets I know. And by the taste of this earth
beneath the rain, I distinguish the place where I am.

LANDSCAPE

to Luis Bustamente

All of a sudden the sky turned orange
and the clouds began to crack
against an intense blue background.
Later it seemed like everything was burning
and over the black hills
that had been invisible
we saw some red ash falling.

CIUDAD TOMADA

> Ellos deambulan en la noche
> de las ciudades.
> Georg Heym

Se sabe que vienen cuando agudos chillidos
invaden la frágil calma de las casas.
Los dormidos se agitan en su sueño
se perturba el destino de los pájaros en vuelo,
los amantes quedan absortos mirando el cielorraso,
a los niños les nacen grandes ojos inmóviles.
Los ancianos no han logrado conciliar el sueño,
en vano evocan otras imágenes de horror
para oponer al presente.
Ha mucho no se lee en la ciudad
los libros ardieron en piras fantásticas
y ante toda letra escrita
los habitantes bajan la vista
llenos de confusión y vergüenza.
Se han visto seres hasta ahora nunca vistos
mirando obscenamente a las jóvenes que se apresuran
antes que se retiren los últimos rayos de un
vago sol
y la sábana negra envuelva la ciudad
y comience la nocturna danza.

CAPTURED CITY

"They wander in the night
of the cities."
Georg Heym

You know they're coming when sharp cries
invade the houses' fragile peace.
Those who are asleep toss and turn in their dreams,
the flying birds lose their way,
lovers stare at the ceiling,
children's eyes open wide in fear.
The old people still don't trust their dreams.
In vain they evoke other images of horror
to oppose the present.
For a long time, nothing has been read in the city.
Books burned in fantastic pyres.
And when the inhabitants see anything written
they lower their eyes
in confusion and shame.
Beings never seen before
look obscenely at girls who run away
before the last rays
of a vague sun fade
and the black sheet covers the city
and the nocturnal dance begins.

LOS DÍAS DEL POETA

En los días de su vida
hubo acontecimientos tristes
y amables.
El cielo cambió de color muchas veces
y la lluvia del sur
-rencorosa-
lavó cada invierno
la tierra que él lamió en su infancia.
Veloces máquinas surcaron el espacio
más allá de los sueños
y del mar surgieron objetos encantados
que guardó con amor.
Dio la vuelta al mundo en grandes barcos
y cruzó a caballo la Cordillera de los Andes
en otro tiempo de tinieblas.
Acontecimientos raros y bellos presenció.
Se fotografió en lugares con nombres exóticos
(es posible recordarlo con una camiseta listada
un gorro
una pipa).
Aparecía y desaparecía en su país de flores y vino
pero el día de su muerte
fue un día oscuro y frío
rodeado de otros días oscuros y fríos.
Un país feamente agrietado se le aleja.
Qué vieron sus ojos pequeños y ávidos
por última vez:
toda la poesía sumida en un pozo,
o el fuego devorando ciudades,
o los hombres diluyéndose como sombras de sombras
mientras un río turbio precipita su cólera animal.
En los días de su vida hubo acontecimientos
tristes y amables,
ocurrieron muchas cosas hermosas
y otras
imposibles de comprender.

THE POET'S DAYS

During the days of his life
sad things happened
as well as some pleasant things.
The sky changed color many times
and the angry rain
in the south
each winter washed
the earth that he put in his mouth as a child.
Rapid machines furrowed space
beyond dreams
and the sea tossed magic objects
onto the beach and he collected them with love.
He went around the world in great ships
and crossed the Andes on horseback
in another time of darkness.
He witnessed strange and beautiful events.
There are photographs of him in places
with exotic names. (It's possible to remember him
in a striped shirt
a cap
        with a pipe.)
He appeared and disappeared in his country
of flowers and wine
but the day of his death
was a dark and cold day
surrounded by other dark and cold days.
A country covered with ugly cracks slips away from him.
What did his small, avid eyes see
toward the end?
all poetry sinking in a well,
or fire devouring cities,
or men dissolving like shadows of shadows
while a dirty river brings on his animal rage.
During the days of his life sad things
happened as well as some pleasant things,
many beautiful things
and others
impossible to understand.

ASEDIO

Mira donde pones el ojo
cazador
lo que ahora no ves
ya nunca más existirá
lo que ahora no toques
enmohecerá
lo que ahora no sientas
te ha de herir algún día.

LOS PÁJAROS SE HAN IDO

Los pájaros se han ido y oscurecen el cielo
estremecidas bandadas pesadas de adioses
se olvidan algunos de mover las alas
y caen a tierra firme
pesados
a tierra firme!
Fueron los años venideros los más turbios de todo
el arcoiris
llovían palabras humedecidas por un largo trayecto
llenas las palabras de plumas de pájaros moribundos
desteñidas horribles hediondas plumas mojadas.
No era un mundo que se deshacía
no era un mundo que se debatía
eran apenas las plumas de torpes pájaros
engañados por las estaciones
abrumados por vientos contrarios
seducidos por las señas que hicimos desde abajo.

SIEGE

Take a good look around,
hunter.
What you don't see now
will never exist again.
What you don't touch now
will turn to dust.
What you don't feel now
will wound you someday.

THE BIRDS HAVE GONE

The birds have gone and darken the sky.
The flocks tremble under the weight of their farewell.
Some of the birds forget to move their wings
and plummet to the hard earth
heavily
to the hard earth.
The coming years were the most turbulent of all
the rainbow.
Moist words rained as long as the journey,
words filled with the feathers of dying birds,
horrible, fading feathers, rank and damp.
It wasn't a world falling apart
or a world still shaken—
just the feathers of lazy birds
deceived by seasons,
overcome by crosswinds,
seduced by our gestures below.

DIARIO DE VIAJE (selecciones)

No es que he llegado tarde
(ni temprano ni tarde)
he llegado en el aire y he quedado en el aire,
me hacen señales que interpreto bien.
En mi pueblo los mapuches invocan a la lluvia
y una cabeza vuela —solitaria— en la noche.

*   *   *

en todas las ciudades de la tierra
llueve
y no puedo dar la cara al cielo
para preguntar a esas nubes
si vienen de los cielos de una ciudad
donde una vez
levanté la cara hacia la lluvia
para preguntarle a las nubes
si venían de los cielos de una ciudad

*   *   *

El reflejo de su rostro en el estanque
es un prodigio de la imaginación

Carne de peregrino.

DESEOS

Unos quieren partir,
otros quieren quedarse para siempre,
en la soledad de las noches unos quieren morir,
otros tiemblan ante la sola idea de la muerte,
unos quieren volver a sus amigos,
otros piensan en el vino y en una tarde de otoño.
Todos quisieran ser dioses o pájaros.

TRAVEL JOURNAL (selections)

It's not that I'm late,
(not early, not late either)
I've arrived in the air and remained in the air.
When they signal me I know what they mean.
In my village, the *mapuche* Indians invoke the rain
and a solitary head flies through the night.

*   *   *

In all the cities on earth
it's raining
and I can't look at the sky
to ask those clouds
if they're coming from the skies of a city
where once
I lifted my face
toward the rain
to ask the clouds
if they were coming from the skies of a city . . .

*   *   *

The reflection of his face in the pond
is a prodigy of the imagination:

the wanderer's flesh.

WISHING

Some want to leave,
others want to stay forever.
In the nights' solitude some want to die,
others tremble at the very thought of death.
Some want to go back to their friends,
others think about wine and an autumn afternoon.
They all wish they were gods or birds.

JUAN LUIS MARTÍNEZ

(1942)

The publication in 1977 of Juan Luis Martínez's first book, *La nueva novela*, marked a fundamental change in recent Chilean poetry. The boundaries of poetry as a literary genre were suddenly destroyed. Or were they amplified? *La nueva novela* creates a complex spatial relationship between the printed word and the visual image through graphic eclecticism and a vast game of intertextuality. Dialectical pairs and contradictory axioms underlie Martínez's work and link it to Chinese poetry, Taoist thought and, in a more contemporary vein, the vertical poetry of Roberto Juarróz from Argentina. Although the lyrical voice disappears in the text along with the author's name scratched out on the cover, the poet's identity is reaffirmed by its very absence. A new logic operates in *La nueva novela* as if the reader were wandering in Lewis Carroll's frustrating and amusing labyrinths. Martínez's absurd and surrealistic world has its own insistent technicalities and rules which must be obeyed.

La poesía chilena, published in 1978, stretches the concept of the book even further in that it contains neither text nor verbal language as they exist in the conventional sense. It consists of authentic reproductions of the death certificates of Gabriela Mistral, Pablo Neruda, Pablo de Rokha and Vicente Huidobro. Each certificate is attached to an index card from a library's card catalogue on which is written a reference to an appropriately funereal text by each poet. Thirty-three blank cards covered by as many Chilean flags make up the bulk of the book which ends with the death certificate of the poet's own father. The book is packaged in its own coffin-like box with a small plastic bag of dirt from Chile's central valley.

Juan Luis Martínez lives with his family in Viña del Mar where, the poet claims, his life has been reduced to an area of three blocks.

LA IDENTIDAD

El niño que yo era
se extravió en el bosque
y ahora el bosque tiene mi edad.

Jean Tardieu à quatre ans

Tardieu, el niño que se observa en la fotografía no es Usted, sino su pequeño hijo que ha desaparecido. A fin de averiguar en qué casa, calle o ciudad volverá a encontrarlo, continúe con el pensamiento o la memoria, el jardín que ciertamente debe prolongarse más allá de los bordes recortados de esta fotografía.

THE IDENTITY

The child I was
got lost in the woods
and now the woods are as old as I am.

Jean Tardieu à quatre ans

Tardieu, the child observed in the photograph, is not you. Rather, it is your small son who has disappeared. In order to discover in which house, street or city you will find him again, pursue by means of thought or memory the garden that without a doubt must extend beyond the cut borders of this photograph

EL TEOREMA DEL JARDIN

a M. Blanchot

Le peintre Victor Tardieu, père du poète

Le peintre Victor Tardieu, père du poète

(La fotografía del niño que aparece en la página 30 y la fotografía de su padre,
que observamos aquí, logran sólo revelar parte de esa extraña relación que pudiera existir a veces entre el espacio de la ficción y los personajes de la vida).

Supongamos que más allá de los bordes recortados de la primera fotografía, el
afuera del jardín se prolonga aquí: en el adentro de este libro.

Imaginemos que en la línea precisa del óvalo (perfecto) de la segunda fotografía, este adentro se cierra sobre sí mismo, dando un límite a ese afuera del jardín, o bien, haciéndolo visible en el espacio que media entre los bordes de una
fotografía y los de la otra: un jardín que no existe como no sea en las pági-
nas de un libro, el que al abrirse, cerró posiblemente ese mismo jardín y que
cerrándose pudiera tal vez volver a abrirlo, borrando así la distancia que existe entre un personaje y el otro.

THE THEOREM OF THE GARDEN

to M. Blanchot

Le peintre / Victor Tardieu, père du poète

Le peintre Victor Tardieu, père du poète

(The photograph of the child that appears on page 31 and the photograph of his father that we observe here succeed in revealing only a part of that strange relationship that might exist sometimes between the space of fiction and the characters of life).

Let's suppose that beyond the cut borders of the first photograph what's outside the garden is extended here: in what's inside this book.

Let's imagine that in the precise line of the (perfect) oval of the second photograph this inside closes upon itself, giving a limit to that outside of the garden, or making it visible in the space that mediates between the borders of one photograph and those of another: a garden that can only exist in the pages of a book, which when opened, might have closed that same garden and when closed might perhaps open it again, thus erasing the distance that exists between one character and another.

ADOLF HITLER Y LA METAFORA DEL CUADRADO

> "La muerte es un maestro de Alemania".
>
> Paul Celan

En este pequeño cuadrado, lo de fuera: (el espacio blanco de la página) y lo de dentro: (la fotografía) están prontos a invertirse, a trocar su hostilidad. Si hay una superficie límite entre tal adentro y tal afuera, dicha superficie es dolorosa en ambos lados.

Mientras aún vivía, A. Hitler pudo sufrir alguna vez el vago recuerdo de un vértigo: esa sensación de caída inminente. Quizás el azaroso viaje de su imagen fotográfica hasta esta página y su virtual caída en este pequeño cuadrado, sea la Metáfora Aproximativa de 2 planos: (el plano real por una caída física, vertical y el plano de la realidad y el recuerdo por la horizontal caída imaginaria) que nos permite saber que el Tiempo, como el Espacio, tiene también su ley de gravedad.

ADOLPH HITLER AND THE METAPHOR OF THE SQUARE

"Death is a schoolmaster from Germany".
Paul Celan

In this small square, what's outside: (the white space of the page) and what's inside: (the photograph) will soon be reversed, exchanging their hostility. If there is a surface limit between such an inside and such an outside, said sur-face is painful on both sides.

While he was still alive, A. Hitler could have suffered at some time the vague memory of some dizziness: that sensation of imminent falling. Perhaps the hazardous journey of his photographic image to this page and its virtual fa-lling into this small square are the Approximate Metaphor of 2 planes: (the real plane for a physical, vertical falling and the plane of reality and memory for the imaginary, horizontal falling) that allows us to know that Time, like Space, also has its law of gravity.

II

TANIA SAVICH Y LA FENOMENOLOGIA DE LO REDONDO

"Das Dasein ist rund".
K. Jaspers

Tania no sabía que El Círculo de la Familia es el lugar donde se encierra a los niños, pero sí sabía que en ese mismo Círculo hay también un centro de orden que proteje a la casa contra un desorden sin límites (un orden que no es simplemente geométrico). Tania vio desaparecer un día el círculo de su familia, pero se quedaba aún a sí misma como delicada habitante de otra redondez que ahora invita al lector a acariciar su pequeña fotografía.

A los 10 años le habían dicho: "Tania, la existencia es hermosa", pero en Otro Círculo, más allá del de su familia, su oído con candorosa intuición geométrica ya había escuchado otra voz: "No Tania. Das Dasein ist rund: La existencia es redonda".

II

TANIA SAVICH AND THE PHENOMENOLOGY OF THE ROUND

"Das Dasein ist rund".
K. Jaspers

Tania didn't know that The Family Circle is the place where the children are enclosed, but she did know that in that same Circle there is also a center of order that protects the house against a disorder without limits (an order that is not simply geometric). Tania saw her family circle disappear one day, but she still remained herself like a delicate inhabitant of another roundness which invites the reader now to caress her small photograph.

When she was 10 years old they had told her: "Tania, existence is beautiful." But in Another Circle, outside of her family's, her ear with innocent geometric intuition had already heard another voice: "No, Tania. Das Dasein ist rund: Existence is round."

LA PROBABLE E IMPROBABLE DESAPARICION DE UN GATO
POR EXTRAVIO DE SU PROPIA PORCELANA

a R. I.   *

Ubicado sobre la repisa de la habitación
el gato no tiene ni ha tenido otra tarea
que vigilar día y noche su propia porcelana.

El gato supone que su imagen fue atrapada
y no le importa si por Neurosis o Esquizofrenia
observado desde la porcelana el mundo sólo sea
una Pequeña Cosmogonía de representaciones malignas
y el Sentido de la Vida se encuentre reducido ahora
a vigilar día y noche la propia porcelana.

A través de su gato
la porcelana observa y vigila también
el inmaculado color blanco de sí misma,
sabiendo que para él ese color es el símbolo pavoroso
de infinitas reencarnaciones futuras.

Pero la porcelana piensa lo que el gato no piensa
y cree que pudiendo haber atrapado también en ella
la imagen de una Virgen o la imagen de un Buddha
fue ella la atrapada por la forma de un gato.

En tanto el gato piensa que si él y la porcelana
no se hubieran atrapado simultáneamente
él no tendría que vigilarla ahora
y ella creería ser La Virgen en la imagen de La Virgen
o alcanzar el Nirvana en la imagen del Buddha.

Y es así como gato y porcelana
se vigilan el uno al otro desde hace mucho tiempo
sabiendo que bastaría la distracción más mínima
para que desaparecieran habitación, repisa, gato y porcelana.

---

*   (La casa de R. I. en Chartres de Francia, tiene las paredes, cielo raso,
piso y muebles cubiertos con fragmentos de porcelana rota).

THE PROBABLE AND IMPROBABLE DISAPPEARANCE OF A CAT BY THE MISPLACING OF ITS OWN PORCELAIN

to R. I. *

Located on the room's mantelpiece
the cat doesn't have nor has it had any other work
except to guard day and night its own porcelain.

The cat supposes that its image was trapped
and it doesn't matter whether because of Neurosis or Schizophrenia
that the world observed from the pordelain is only
a Small Cosmogony of malignant representations
and the Meaning of Life finds itself reduced now
to guarding day and night the porcelain itself.

By means of its cat
the porcelain observes and also guards
its own immaculate white color,
knowing that for the cat that color is the frightening symbol
of infinite future reincarnations.

But the porcelain thinks what the cat doesn't think
and believes that having been able to trap in itself
the image of a Virgin or the image of a Buddha
the porcelain was the one who was trapped by the form of a cat.

Meanwhile, the cat thinks that if he and the porcelain
hadn't trapped each other simultaneously
he wouldn't have to guard it now
and it would believe that it was the Virgin in the image of the Virgin
or that it could reach Nirvana in the image of the Buddha.

And this is how cat and porcelain
have been guarding each other for a long time
knowing that the slightest distraction would be enough
to make room, mantelpiece, cat and porcelain disappear.

* (The walls, ceiling, floor and furniture of R. I.'s house in Chartres, France
are covered with pieces of broken porcelain).

EL GATO DE CHESHIRE

"El Nombrar a los Gatos es un asunto difícil".
T. S. Eliot

Suponga que usted es Alicia y pasa una temporada en el País de las Maravillas. Allí encuentra un gato sin cuerpo cuya cabeza flota en el vacío. Este gato aparece y desaparece a voluntad. Este gato descorporizado ostenta una permanente y misteriosa sonrisa. Usted se lo presenta al Rey, pero el Rey no gusta del aspecto de este extraño amigo suyo y decide eliminarlo: El verdugo opina que no se puede cortar una cabeza a menos que exista un cuerpo del cual cortarla. El Rey dice que cualquier cosa que tenga una cabeza puede ser decapitada. ~~BUSQUE UNA SOLUCION.~~

1) Decapitar es separar la cabeza del cuerpo.
Como el gato no tiene cuerpo,
no lo puedo decapitar.

2) Decapitar es cortar la cabeza.
Como el gato tiene cabeza,
entonces usted puede decapitarlo.

1. La naturaleza de este gato-CABEZA impide que su parte anterior-superior — CABEZA, sea separada de su no-cuerpo.

2. El cuerpo del gato:
"Es, pues, más bien una infinidad infinita de no ser". Q...

3. ~~EL GATO ES LA CABEZA~~
~~EL CUERPO ES EL CUERPO~~
O a la inversa
el gato no es la cabeza
ni el cuerpo es el cuerpo
~~O A LA INVERSA~~
~~el cuerpo es el cuerpo~~
~~la cabeza no es el cuerpo~~
o a la inversa . . .

4. ~~El cuerpo del gato está sumergido hasta el cuello~~
~~en la "infinidad del no ser".~~

5. ~~La CABEZA-GATO es VISIBLE~~
~~El NO-CUERPO-No-GATO no es visible~~

6. Que el cuerpo no sea visible,
no significa que el gato no tenga cuerpo.
Que la cabeza no sea invisible,
no significa que el gato tenga cuerpo.

EL CUELLO DEL GATO ES UN PUNTO INDEFINIDO Y VACILANTE ENTRE LO VISIBLE Y LO INVISIBLE.

THE CHESHIRE CAT

"The Naming of Cats is a difficult matter".
T. S. Eliot

Suppose that you are Alice and that you spend some time in Wonderland. There you find a cat without a body whose head floats in the void. This cat appears and disappears at will. This disembodied cat displays a permanent and mysterious smile. You present it to the King, but the King doesn't like the looks of this strange friend of yours and decides to eliminate it: the Executioner is of the opinion that one can't cut off a head unless there's a body from which to cut it off. The King says that anything that has a head can be decapitated. ~~FIND A SOLUTION.~~

1) To decapitate is to separate the head from the body.
   Since the cat doesn't have a body,
   I can't decapitate it.

2) To decapitate is to cut off the head.
   Since the cat has a head,
   you can decapitate it.

1. The nature of this cat-HEAD keeps its anterior-superior-HEAD part from being separated from its non-body.

2. The body of the cat:
   "It is, then, in other words, an infinite infinity of non-being". Q. . .

3. ~~THE CAT IS THE HEAD~~
   ~~THE BODY IS THE BODY~~
   Or the opposite
   the cat isn't the head
   nor is the body the body
   ~~OR THE OPPOSITE~~
   ~~the body is the body~~
   ~~the head isn't the body~~
   or the opposite

4. ~~The body of the cat is submerged to the neck~~
   ~~in the "infinity of non-being".~~

5. ~~The HEAD-CAT is VISIBLE~~
   ~~The NON-BODY Non-CAT isn't visible~~

6. That the body isn't visible
   doesn't mean that the cat doesn't have a body.
   That the head isn't invisible
   doesn't mean that the cat has a body.

THE NECK OF THE CAT IS AN UNDEFINED AND VACILLATING POINT BETWEEN THE VISIBLE AND THE INVISIBLE.

FOX TERRIER DESAPARECE EN LA INTERSECCION DE LAS AVENIDAS GAUSS Y LOBATCHEWSKY *

Suponga que su perrito de raza Fox Terrier, de pelaje a manchas negras sobre fondo blanco y que obedece al nombre de "SOGOL", se dirige por una avenida y al llegar a la esquina de otra, desaparece súbitamente. AVERIGÜE DONDE Y COMO PUEDE VOLVER A ENCONTRARLO.

1.

a. La avenida Gauss sólo es invisible en su punto de intersección con la avenida Lobatchewsky.

b. La avenida Lobatchewsky sólo es visible en su punto de intersección con la avenida Gauss.

2.

a. Que las avenidas Gauss y Lobatchewsky sean invisibles en uno u otro punto de sí mismas, no significa que el Fox Terrier no sea visible en cualquier punto de ambas avenidas.

b. Que el Fox Terrier sea visible en cualquier punto de ambas avenidas, no significa que en la intersección de las 2 avenidas no pueda haber un punto donde el Fox Terrier sea invisible.

c. Si el Fox Terrier se encontrara detenido en la intersección de ambas avenidas, sería visible desde cualquier punto de la avenida Gauss.

d. Si el Fox Terrier se encontrara detenido en la intersección de ambas avenidas, en forma invisible, sería visible desde cualquier punto de la avenida Lobatchewsky.

3.

a. Sólo es posible suponer que el Fox Terrier haya desaparecido en esa fisura precisa e infinitesimal en que se intersectan ambas avenidas.

b. Dado que esa fisura precisa e infinitesimal pertenece a las geometrías no euclidianas la única solución es que el Fox Terrier regrese por sus propios medios desde esa otra dimensión, cuya entrada y salida se encuentra en la intersección de las avenidas Gauss y Lobatchewsky.

---

* "Todas las calles son invisibles. Las visibles son falsas, aunque algunas visibles son la parte final de las invisibles".

Yoko Ono

FOX TERRIER DISAPPEARS AT THE INTERSECTION
OF GAUSS AND LOBATCHEWSKY AVENUES *

Suppose that your little dog of Fox Terrier breed, whose fur is black spots
on a white background and who comes to the name of "SOGOL", is going
along one avenue and suddenly disappears upon arriving at the corner of the
other. FIND OUT WHERE AND HOW YOU CAN FIND HIM AGAIN.

1.
a. Gauss Avenue is only invisible
 in this point of intersection with Lobatchewsky Avenue.

b. Lobatchewsky Avenue is only visible
 in its point of intersection with Gauss Avenue.

2.
a. That Gauss and Lobatchewsky Avenues
 are invisible at one or another point of themselves,
 does not mean that the Fox Terrier is not visible
 at any point of both avenues.

b. That the Fox Terrier is visible
 at any point of both avenues,
 does not mean that at the intersection of the 2 avenues
 there couldn't be a point where the Fox Terrier is invisible.

c. If the Fox Terrier found himself detained
 at the intersection of both avenues,
 he would be visible from any point on Gauss Avenue.

d. If the Fox Terrier found himself detained
 at the intersection of both avenues, in invisible form,
 he would be visible from any point on Lobatchewsky Avenue.

3.
a. It is only possible to suppose that the Fox Terrier
 has disappeared in that precise and infinitesimal fissure
 in which both avenues intersect.

b. Given that that precise and infinitesimal fissure
 belongs to non-Euclidean geometries,
 the only solution is that the Fox Terrier
 return on his own from that other dimension
 whose entrance and exit are found at the intersection
 of Gauss and Lobatchewsky Avenues.

* "All streets are invisible. The visible ones are false, even though some visble ones are
the final part of the invisible ones".
                                        Yoko Ono

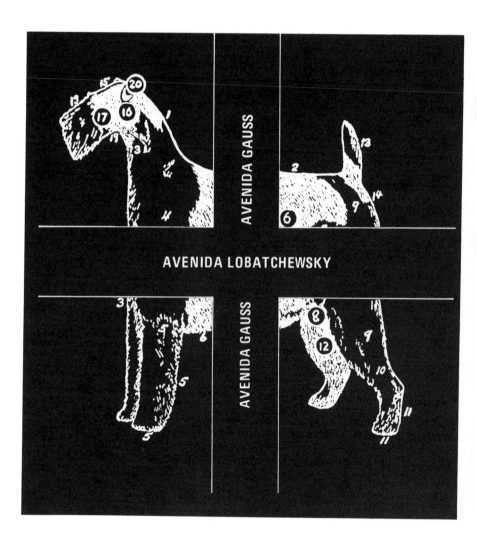

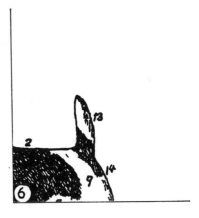
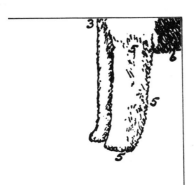
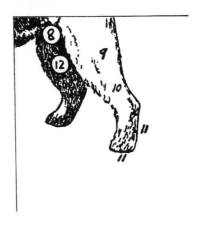

AVENIDA GAUSS

AVENIDA LOBATCHEWSKY

AVENIDA GAUSS

FOX TERRIER NO DESAPARECIDO NO REAPARECE
EN LA NO-INTERSECCION DE LAS NO-AVENIDAS (~~GAUSS Y LOBATCHEWSKY~~)

Suponga que su perrito Fox Terrier es visto por última vez cuando a razón de
un trotecito constante de 10 Kms./Hr. se dirige desde su no-casa hacia la
no-intersección de las no-avenidas donde debe desaparecer. Usted sale tras él
a igual velocidad, realizando la misma trayectoria, pero sin lograr alcanzarlo.
Usted regresa entonces a su no-casa donde advierte que ya han transcurrido
30 minutos desde que el Fox Terrier iniciara su recorrido. CALCULE
EXACTAMENTE LA DISTANCIA QUE HAY ENTRE SU NO-CASA Y LA
NO-INTERSECCION DE LAS NO-AVENIDAS GAUSS Y LOBATCHEWSKY.

1.
a.   Las no-avenidas Gauss y Lobatchwsky
son a tramos igualmente falsas o verdaderas, visibles o invisibles.

b.   Los tramos visibles e invisibles de cualquiera de las 2 no-avenidas
son también los tramos falsos y verdaderos de la otra no-avenida.
(Y viceversa).

2.
a.   En su trayectoria desde la no-casa
hasta la no-intersección de las 2 no-avenidas
el Fox Terrier atraviesa tramos falsos y verdaderos,
tramos visibles y tramos invisibles.

b.   A tramos falsos y verdaderos,
a tramos visibles e invisibles
el Fox Terrier logra cubrir la distancia
que mediaba entre la no-casa y la no-intersección de las 2 no-avenidas.

c.   La trayectoria del Fox Terrier
a través de tramos falsos y tramos verdaderos,
de tramos visibles y tramos invisibles
puede ser también falsa o verdadera, visible o invisible.

d.   Según atravesó en su trayectoria tramos falsos o verdaderos
el Fox Terrier fue un perrito falso o verdadero,
así mismo cuando atravesó tramos visibles o invisibles
el perrito sólo fue un Fox Terrier visible o invisible.

3.
a.   Es posible suponer que el Fox Terrier no haya desaparecido jamás
en esa no-fisura no-precisa ni infinitesimal
en que se intersectan las 2 no-avenidas
(como en ese ningún otro punto donde no se intersectan las 2 no-avenidas).

b.   Dado que esa no-fisura no-precisa ni infinitesimal
no pertenece a las geometrías euclidianas
la única no-solución es que el Fox Terrier no regrese jamás
desde esa otra no-dimensión donde jamás desapareció,
pero cuya entrada y salida seguimos encontrando
en la intersección de las avenidas Gauss y Lobatchewsky.

NON-MISSING FOX TERRIER DOES NOT REAPPEAR
AT THE NON-INTERSECTION OF THE NON-AVENUES (~~GAUSS AND LOBATCHEWSKY~~)

Suppose that your little Fox Terrier is last seen when, at the rate of a constant trot at 10 kms./Hr., he moves from your non-house toward the non-intersection of the non-avenues where he should disappear. You go out after him at the same speed, following the same trajectory, but without being able to reach him. You return then to your non-house where you notice that 30 minutes have gone by since the Fox Terrier began his route. CALCULATE EXACTLY THE DISTANCE BETWEEN YOUR NON-HOUSE AND THE NON-INTERSECTION OF GAUSS AND LOBATCHEWSKY NON-AVENUES.

1.
a. Gauss and Lobatchewsky non-Avenues
   are, in length, equally false or true, visible or invisible.

b. The visible and invisible lengths of either 2 non-avenues
   are also the false and true lengths of the other non-avenue.
   (And vice versa).

2.
a. In his trajectory from the non-house
   to the non-intersection of the 2 non-avenues,
   the Fox Terrier false and true lengths,
   visible lengths and invisible lengths.

b. By false and true lengths,
   by visible and invisible lenghts,
   the Fox Terrier succeeds in covering the distance
   that was in the middle between the non-house
   and the non-intersection of the 2 non-avenues.

c. The trajectory of the Fox Terrier
   along false lengths and true lengths,
   visible lengths and invisible lengths
   can also be false or true, visible or invisible.

d. According to the way he crossed false or true lengths in his trajectory,
   the Fox Terrier was a false or true little dog,
   likewise when he crossed visible or invisible lengths
   the little dog was only a visible or invisible Fox Terrier.

3.
a. It is possible to suppose that the Fox Terrier has never disappeared
   in that non-precise, non-infinitesimal non-fissure
   in which the two non-avenues intersect
   (as in that no other point where the 2 non-avenues do not intersect).

b. Given that that non-precise, non-infinitesimal non-fissure
   does not belong to Euclidean geometries,
   the only non-solution is that the Fox Terrier never return
   from that other non-dimension where he never disappeared,
   but whose entrance and exit we continue to find
   at the intersection of Gauss and Lobatchewsky Avenues.

JAIME QUEZADA

(1942)

The majority of Jaime Quezada's poetry is centered on the family, the home and the objects that surrounded the poet as a boy in Los Angeles, Chile. The nostalgic search in the poems for a lost utopian world of revelatory landscapes links Quezada's work with that of his compatriot, Jorge Teillier, from the Generation of 1950. Referred to in Chile as *la poesía lárica*, this kind of poetry is associated with writers from the southern part of the country. The mysticism and prophetic qualities of Quezada's recently published book, *Huerfanías*, maintain the poet's alliance with the land, whether it is the coast, the Nahuelbuta mountain range or some other remote corner of Chile's geography where Quezada, an incessant, solitary wanderer, travels. Quezada was a founder of the literary group called Arúspice in Concepción and is now living in Santiago where he writes for the magazines *Ercilla* and *Paula*.

POEMA DE LAS COSAS OLVIDADAS

El caracol blanco en la playa vacío
Y llenándose de arena
como si fuese un antiguo reloj
señalando la edad del viento

El largo tren sin silencio
como un ídolo sonoro
moviéndose en los rieles oscuros
Y la estación vacía
No hay tiempo para esperar al viejo viajero

El sol abierto como una nuez roja
despertando el principio de toda mariposa
Y nunca ilumina
el cuarto vacío de mi madre pobre

Tantas cosas olvidadas
Y existiendo más que el hombre.

POEM OF THE FORGOTTEN THINGS

The white seashell on the beach
empty and filling itself with sand
as if it were an old watch
signalling the wind's age

The long train without silence
like a resonant idol
moving on dark rails
And the empty station
There's no time to wait for the old traveler

The open sun like a red walnut
awakening the beginning of all butterflies
And it never shines
in the empty room of my poor mother

So many forgotten things
that last longer than man.

EL COMETA HALLEY

En el verano de 1910 el cometa Halley
aparéció en los cielos de Chile
Ese mismo año murió el presidente Pedro Montt
En 1758 hubo una lluvia de aerolitos
Y piedras de fuego quemaron los muchos bosques
del verde territorio
También una sequía en 1834
Y una plaga de ratas y ratones asoló campos y graneros
al igual que en el verano de 1986
Sólo que ahora incluyendo cárceles secretas
cuarteles estadios de fútbol conventos y ciudades
(Y la muerte del presidente)

En el año de 2062 el cometa Halley
aparecerá otra vez en los cielos de Chile
Para entonces yo Jaime Quezada
sobreviviente chozno de tanta historia
Estaré a la sombra de una nube atómica
Rascándome con una teja en medio de la ceniza
O muy sentado en una mecedora silla de neutrones
A la sombra de un nuevo manzano en flor
Recordando la infancia de mi padre
Cuando se hacía retratar bajando de un caballo en 1910.

HALLEY'S COMET

In the summer of 1910 Halley's comet
      appeared in the skies of Chile
That same year President Pedro Montt died
In 1758 meteorites rained down
And stones of fire burned the many forests
             of the green territory
There was also a drought in 1834
And a plague of rats and mice devastated fields and granaries
      just like the summer of 1986
Only now including secret jails
    barracks soccer stadiums convents and cities
(And the death of the president)

In the year 2062 Halley's comet
    will appear again in the skies of Chile
At that time I Jaime Quezada
           survivor of so much history
Will be in the shadow of an atomic cloud
Scratching myself with what's left of a rooftop amidst the ash
Or sitting down in a rocking chair of neutrons
In the shade of a new apple tree in bloom
Remembering my father's childhood
When a picture was taken of him getting off a horse in 1910.

ASÍ DE COSAS DE ARRIBA COMO DE ABAJO

Parece que suena un teléfono en medio del campo
O un eco de montaña en la ciudad muerta:
Escucho clarito que alguien me llama por mi nombre
Subo al techo de una casa antigua
Y sólo quiebro tejas
A un árbol frutal de un patio vecino
Y tres veces un centinela pregunta quién vive
Al último peldaño de una escala telescópica
Y hay llamas como de incendio
A la terraza de un edificio de veinticinco pisos
Y una paloma está muerta si de esmog si de pólvora
Al punto más alto de la cordillera de Nahuelbuta
Y veo nubes puras nubes

No encuentro huella alguna
Tengo hambre
Tengo sed
Quiero por fin subir a un madero en un camino rural
Y el madero está ocupado por un hombre moribundo
No vuela un pájaro

Me siento más solo que nunca
No sé de veras qué hacer:
No me llamaba alguien hace un rato por mi nombre?
Formo corneta con mis manos
Saco pañuelos
Grito a todo pulmón mi santo y seña
       mi estatura mis brazos abiertos
Y me voy sin esperanza a un establo cercano

Hago fuego
Ordeño una vaca
Me siento a ras de suelo a beber un poco de leche
De mi barba cae un pelo (igual
       como cae de un ciruelo una hoja) a la jarra caliente
Y el pelo es en la leche un rayo de sol.

THE WAY THINGS ARE ABOVE AND BELOW

It sounds like a phone ringing in the middle of the countryside
Or a mountain echo in the dead city:
I hear someone call me clearly by my name
I go out on the roof of an ancient house
And I only break the tiles
I climb a fruit tree in a neighboring patio
And three times a watchman asks Who goes there
I go up the last step of a telescopic stairway
And there are flames
I go out on the terrace of a twenty-five story building
And a dove is dead either from smog or gunpowder
I climb the highest point of the mountain range near Nahuelbuta
And I see clouds and more clouds
I don't find a single trail
I'm hungry
I'm thirsty
Finally I feel like climbing a wooden beam on a country road
And the wooden beam is occupied by a dying man
Not a single bird flies

I feel more alone than ever
I really don't know what to do:
Wasn't someone calling me by my name just now
I cup my hands around my mouth
I wave handkerchiefs
I shout my vital statistics at the top of my lungs
              with open arms my height
And I go without hope to a nearby stable

I make a fire
I milk a cow
I sit on the ground and drink a little milk
A hair falls from my beard (just
       like a leaf falls from a plumtree) into the warm bucket
And the hair in the milk is a ray of sunlight.

EL SILBO DE LOS AIRES

Se me confunde Haendel un afervoroso día
Con el sonido supersónico de un avión
Hawker Hunter más arriba de las nubes
Y no sé si es trompeta apocalíptica
el sonido que del cielo viene
O barroco aire de órgano el que sube.

DESPERTAR

Mientras todos
caminan con los cántaros
vacíos en sus hombros:
el agua corre
perforando la tranquilidad de las piedras

Mas la niebla
cada mañana baja por el cerro
Y envuelve al hombre
Y lo desnuda
hasta dejarlo sin palabras.

WHISTLING IN THE AIR

One listless day I confused Handel
with the sound of a supersonic
    Hawker Hunter jet higher than the clouds
And I didn't know if it was the apocalyptic
        blast of trumpets—
the sound coming down from the sky—
or the baroque air of the organ rising.

WAKING UP

While everyone
walks with empty
jugs on their shoulders
the water runs
perforating the tranquil stones

But the fog
each morning comes down from the mountain
And envelops man
And strips him
leaving him without words

MANUEL SILVA ACEVEDO

(1942)

The savage and pacific extremes of human nature, embodied in the conventional symbols of the wolf and the sheep, are the moral focus of Silva Acevedo's most well-known work, *Lobos y ovejas*. In this book, the poet explores the psychological contradictions and dark longings carried to more violent levels in *Mester de bastardía*. The genre of love poetry in his book, *Monte de Venus*, takes on a new dimension where brutality and affection are mysteriously joined. Manuel Silva often relies on the technique of enumeration in his work and, as a result, the poem must define itself on the basis of the preponderance of metaphor or a series of ostensibly unrelated images as seen by the poet. Silva Acevedo's poetry has been translated into four languages and two of his five books have received prizes in Chile.

The poet works in Santiago in an advertising agency.

A LA MANERA DE APOLLINAIRE

Así te quiero
paridora como coneja
criminal como víbora
tiránica como abeja
inescrupulosa como hiena
voraz como la rata de afilados dientes
pequeña como el piojo de la harina
impertinente como los cuervos de las fábulas
sabia como la más necia de las criaturas
obvia como el cielo
rapaz como la garra de la buha
ardiente como la loba en celo
sigilosa como las bacterias
venenosa como ciertos hongos
impaciente como las cigarras
rápida como la lengua del basilisco
triste como la lluvia
humilde como la cabeza entre las manos
fugaz como las estrellas fugaces
permanente como el silencio
alba como las estrellas multitudinarias
frágil como una moneda
desnuda como las estatuas y más que las estatuas
abierta como las flores abierta hasta el delirio
colmada como colmena en el verano
profusa como las primeras letras
confiada como las golondrinas en los cables eléctricos
desconfiada como los sepultureros
sagaz como las nutrias
dramática como las manos del mudo
sonora como la música en la cabeza del sordo
adorable como la costa para el náufrago
increíble como las puertas abiertas de una cárcel
celestial como las llamas crepitantes
infernal como la quemadura de la nieve
cruel como yo
te quiero con locura de sabio
empecinado en sus cálculos inútiles
mi signo mi dibujo mi libro recién impreso
pequeña ola de río
quilla rompiendo mis espumas
te quiero

À LA APOLLINAIRE

I love you when you're
fertile like a rabbit
criminal like a snake
tyrannical like a bee
unscrupulous like a hyena
voracious like a sharp-toothed rat
small like lice in flour
impertinent like the crows of fables
wise like the most foolish of creatures
obvious like the sky
greedy like an owl's talons
burning like the she-wolf in heat
stealthy like bacteria
poisonous like certain mushrooms
impatient like grasshoppers
rapid like the basilisk's tongue
sad like the rain
humble like your head between your hands
fleeting like the fleeting stars
permanent like silence
white like the multitudinous stars
fragile like a coin
naked like the statues and more than the statues
open like flowers opening into delirium
spilling over like a summer beehive
abundant like learning to write
confident like swallows on electric wires
suspicious like gravediggers
clever like otters
dramatic like the hands of a mute
vibrant like the music in a deaf man's head
welcomed like the coast seen by a shipwrecked sailor
incredible like the open doors of a jail
blue like the center of crackling flames
infernal like burning snow
cruel like me
I love you with the madness of a wise man
persistent in his useless calculations
my mark my portrait my book just published
small wave of the river
keel crashing through my surf
I love you

LOBOS Y OVEJAS *(fragmentos)*

Yo, la oveja soñadora,
pacía entre las nubes
Pero un día la loba me tragó
Y yo, la estúpida cordera,
conocí entonces la noche
la verdadera noche
Y allí en la tiniebla
de su entraña de loba
me sentí lobo malo de repente

*   *   *

El lobo dio alcance a la loba
Yo lo estaba viendo
La cogió de los flancos con el hocico
Lamió su vientre y aulló
irguiendo la cabeza
Yo lo estaba viendo
Yo que no soy más que una oveja asustadiza
Y puedo afirmarlo nuevamente
El lobo y la loba lloraban
restregando sus cuellos
La oscuridad les caía encima
Había un gran silencio
No había más que piedras
y los astros rodaban por el cielo

*   *   *

Se engaña el pastor
Se engaña el propio lobo
No seré más la oveja en cautiverio
El sol de la llanura
calentó demasiado mi cabeza
Me convertí en la fiera milagrosa
Ya tengo mi lugar entre las fieras
Ampárate pastor, ampárate de mí
Lobo en acecho, ampárame

WOLVES AND SHEEP (fragments)

I was the sheep who loved to daydream
and graze among the clouds
But one day I was swallowed by the wolf
And being the stupid lamb I was,
then I knew the night
the true night
And there in the darkness
of the wolf's guts
I suddenly felt like a bad wolf

*   *   *

The wolf drew near his mate
I was watching
He closed his mouth on her flanks
licked her belly and howled
lifting his head
I was watching
even though I'm nothing more than a frightened sheep
And it's true what I saw
the two wolves were crying
rubbing against each other's necks
Darkness fell upon them
There was a great silence
Nothing more than stones
and stars wheeling through the sky

*   *   *

The shepherd is mistaken
Even the wolf is mistaken
I won't be the captive sheep any more
The prairie sun
made me think a little too much
I turned into the miraculous wild beast
I already have my place among the other beasts
Hide, shepherd, hide yourself from me
Wolf lying in ambush, give me shelter

DANUBIO AZUL

Era un animal romántico, dijo el orangután
y apretó en su puño al granadero
y luego lo engulló
y se llenó de cintas de primera comunión
de fragatas en llamas
de bosques azotados por vendavales
de pequeñas explosiones atómicas
de cadáveres en campos de batalla.

Era un animal mitológico, dijo la hiena
sumida en las tripas del orangután
y se sintió repleta de medallas y escarapelas
de ofrendas florales y salvas de cañonazos
de asonadas callejeras y cargas de caballería
de marchas nupciales interrumpidas a balazos.

Era vox populi un animal de mala entraña, dijo el gusano
royendo las entrañas podridas de la hiena
y entonces fue el Día del Juicio Final
y los cadáveres diseminados en campos de batalla
se pusieron de pie
y estalló el Danubio Azul
y cada oveja tomó a su pareja
y se danzó hasta altas horas de la madrugada
hasta que la multitud derribó las puertas de Palacio
y una pálida dama desmayándose en los brazos de su granadero
exclamó: es el siglo que muere, amor mío.

BLUE DANUBE

I used to be a romantic animal, said the orangutan
squeezing the grenadier in his fist
and then gulping him down
filling himself with first communion ribbons
frigates in flames
forests whipped by gusts of wind
small atomic explosions
bodies on battlefields

I used to be a mythological animal, said the hyena
wading in the orangutan's guts
and feeling full with all the medals and decorations
offerings of flowers and salvos of cannons
massive protest in the streets and charging cavalry
wedding marches interrupted by gunfire.

I used to be *vox populi*, rotten to the core, said the worm,
eating the rancid entrails of the hyena.
And then it was the Day of the Last Judgment
and the corpses strewn over battlefields
stood up
and the Blue Danube exploded
and every sheep found its mate
and there was dancing until dawn
until the multitude broke down the Palace doors
and a pale lady fainting in her grenadier's arms
exclaimed: it's the dying century, my love.

ME HAN ROTO EL HUESO MÁS FINO DEL OÍDO

Veo trotar los percherones de un carro funerario
en silencio absoluto
Veo un caballero que mueve los labios
y no le entiendo nada
Veo a un pariente mío conteniendo la risa
    en la sala de baño
Veo un traje vacío colgado del ropero
Veo una banda de músicos sepultada en la nieve.

REACCIÓN EN CADENA

Un inocente paseo por el bosque
puede llegar a convertirse
en una implacable cacería
Un inofensivo intercambio de miradas
puede desatar la reacción en cadena
la desintegración total de la materia
Bailamos al filo de la medianoche
Danzamos sobre un campo minado
Besaría su boca con pasión brutal
pero el riesgo es incalculable

THEY'VE BROKEN THE MOST DELICATE BONE IN MY EAR

I see the horses of a funeral carriage
trot by in absolute silence
I see a gentleman moving his lips
and I don't understand anything he says
I see a relative of mine holding in his laughter
in the bathroom
I see an empty suit hanging in the closet
I see a group of musicians buried in snow.

CHAIN REACTION

An innocent walk through the woods
can turn into
an implacable hunt
A harmless exchange of looks
can set off the chain reaction
the total disintegration of matter
We step to the edge of midnight
We dance over the minefield
I'd kiss your mouth with brutal passion
but the risk is incalculable

WALDO ROJAS

(1943)

Waldo Rojas's book, *El puente oculto (The Hidden Bridge)*, published in Spain in 1980, is a good example of how some of the young poets living in exile have attempted to re-evaluate their work by joining, in the form of personal anthologies, poems written before and after leaving Chile. While the themes vary in the selection of poems written by Rojas between 1966 and 1980, the strange artificial span of language in *El puente oculto* has remained a constant. The disassociation of the poetic word from the object described is part of the expressive technique that Waldo Rojas has defined as "a system of obsessions." What is poetic is not located in things but in a certain capacity of the language itself. Rojas's poetry is not the conversational "anti-poetry" of Nicanor Parra. It is filled with archaic, unusual and Latinate words that are often arranged in a difficult syntax. There is a certain baroque pleasure on the part of the poet in the careful elaboration of each poem's dense, subjective reality.

Rojas lives and teaches in Paris.

AJEDREZ

Antonius Block jugaba al ajedrez con la Muerte junto al mar.
sobre la arena salpicada de alfiles y caballos derrotados.
Su escudero Juan, mientras tanto, contaba con los dedos las jugadas,
sin saberlo,
en la creencia de que lo que contaba eran peregrinos de una extraña
caravana

(Y a mi que no me gusta el ajedrez sino en raras
circunstanciás.
Yo, que pude luego de perder estruendosamente una partida
beberme una botella con el ganador y sostenerle el puño en alto.)

Pero Antonius Block sin duda era un eximio ajedrecista
no obstante haber perdido el último partido de su vida.
Antonius Block, quien volvía de las Cruzadas, no tuvo en cuenta
que a Dios no le habría gustado el ajedrez
aún cuando de veras hubiera algún día existido.

Afortunadamente todo esto sucedía en una sala de cine.
El mundo en miniatura en tres metros cuadrados a lo más.
Los otros personajes han pagado las consecuencias al terminar
la función.

Sería bueno sostener ahora que el ajedrez está algo pasado de moda.
A pesar de la costumbre por los símbolos
y de los cuadraditos blancos y negros irreconciliables
en que se debate la vida
*   a coletazos.*

CHESS

Antonius Block played chess with Death at seaside
on the sand sprinkled with bishops and routed knights.
His squire, John, meanwhile, was counting the moves
on his fingers without knowing it
in the belief that what he was counting were pilgrims
from a strange caravan.

(And I'm someone who doesn't like chess
except on rare occasions.
Right after noisily losing a game,
I could drink a bottle with the winner
and lift his fist in the air.)

But Antonius Block was, without a doubt, a superior chess player
despite having lost the last match for his life.
Antonius Block, who was returning from the Crusades,
didn't take into account
that·God wouldn't have liked chess
even though, in truth, it would have existed someday.

Fortunately, all this happened in a movie theatre.
The world in miniature on nine square feet at most.
The other characters paid the consequences when the show was over.
It would be good to maintain that chess is sort of passé.
In spite of our habits, symbols
and the black and white irreconcilable little squares
where life trembles
                    until the tail twitches for the last time.

CALLE

Todos los caminos conducen a esta calle que se mira a sí misma
a través de sus ventanas.
Todos los pasos alejan de esta calle
y es su soledad lo único que crece en la medida de
las luces
y del pestañear de alas de murciélagos.
Haremos algo alguna vez en esta calle que no sea caminar

y blanquearnos los hombros con la cal de sus muros,
aunque es ésta la Calle de los Pasos que se Esfuman
con la velocidad del resonar del empedrado de su suelo.

Es ésta la calle que se fuga de su imagen,
que tambalea sin caer en el recuerdo
y es en ella donde habita —desterrado—
"aquél extraño que en ciertos momentos viene a nuestro
encuentro en un espejo."

AQUÍ SE CIERRA EL CÍRCULO

Aquí se cierra el círculo:
        el crujido esperado se produce
aunque en el peor momento, y nos llena de escombros las orejas.
En adelante habrá un adentro y un afuera en todas partes.
Un adentro debajo de la tierra,
un afuera lejos de la curva del planeta.
Un afuera terrible, flotando en un satélite,
y un adentro sin sonido, hueco, tres metros bajo el suelo.

STREET

All roads lead to this street looking at itself
through its windows.
All footsteps recede from this street
and its solitude is all that grows
beneath the lights
and the blinking of bats' wings.
Someday we'll do something in this street
besides walking and getting the white chalk
from the walls on our shoulders,
even though this is the Street of Vanishing Footsteps
that disappear with the echoes they make on the cobbled streets.

This is the street that flees its image,
that topples without falling in memory
and it's where someone lives in exile—
"that strange person who sometimes comes to meet us
in a mirror."

THE CIRCLE CLOSES HERE

The circle closes here:
            there's the creaking noise we waited for
even though it comes at the worst time and fills our ears with rubble.
From now on, there will be an inside and an outside everywhere.
An inside beneath the earth,
an outside far from the curve of the planet.
A terrible outside, floating in a satellite,
and an inside without sound, hollow, six feet under the ground.

NO ENTREGAREMOS LA NOCHE*

*Pero qué sueño es éste a cuya orilla me dejan
como a la espera de un cuerpo prometido por las aguas,
cuasi réplica de mí, desdoblamiento brumoso,
a las puertas de mi propio cuerpo llamando sin respuesta,
cual un bocado salivado en demasía,
artífice de un asco convocado por mí mismo.
Leo en la oscuridad una escritura de tientos,
tacto de sangre en espumas, sin peso,
y es así como me viene a herir el día,
lo respiro, sin embargo, aspiro, exhalo,
más bien me hallo mordiendo con hambre la blandura
de la luz solar
que en los objetos revive un estupor sin culpas,
y eso es como si fuera inoculando en el corazón del Miedo
un bálsamo ferviente de arena tibia.*

·

*Escrito en Santiago de Chile durante las primeras semanas consecutivas al golpe de estado de septiembre de 1973. El título está basado en una célebre frase del General Leigh, ex-miembro de la Junta de Gobierno, justificando la prolongación del estricto toque de queda: "No entregaremos la noche a esos terroristas emboscados que amenazan la vida de nuestros soldados . . ."

WE WILL NOT HAND OVER THE NIGHT*

But what dream is this on whose shore they leave me
as if I were waiting for a body promised by the waters,
quasi-double of myself, unfolding of fog,
at the doors of my own body calling with no answer,
like a morsel covered with too much saliva,
craftsman of some nausea I convoked myself.
I read the writings in darkness by feel,
touch of blood in surf, weightless,
and that's the way the day comes to wound me,
I breathe it in, nevertheless, inhaling, exhaling,
I discover I'm hungry and chew on the soft
solar light
that revives in objects a guiltless stupor,
and it's as if it were inoculating
a fervent balsam of warm sand
in the heart of Fear.

---

*Written in September, 1973, after the military coup. The title is based on the
words of General Leigh, ex-member of the military junta, as he justified the
continuing of a strict curfew: "We will not hand over the night to those
terrorists who threaten the lives of our soldiers."

ROTTERDAM

Gaviotas sobre la espesura
de mástiles metálicos,
aves tumultuosas de todos los augurios
sobrevuelan el naufragio silencioso del agua
en la tortuosa inmovilidad del hierro.

HÔTEL DE LA GARE

Breve tregua de la noche de presa en la Ciudad Terminal
esta oscuridad estrecha y desconocida de ambos.
Con un miedo cierto del tacto de sus voces
un cuerpo llama al otro en esta manera de abrazo
fatigante y calmador.
Ni una palabra que agite, entonces, el aire que se llaga:

separación de sus cuerpos.

Y son ahora dos mitades arduamente mutuas
como en el brillo de la hoja del cuchillo rebanador
se contemplan sin sorpresa
los hemisferios de fresca pulpa del fruto dividido.

ROTTERDAM

Gulls over the thickness
of metal masts,
tumultuous birds of all omens
flying over the silent shipwreck
of the water
in the twisting immobility of iron.

HÔTEL DE LA GARE

The brief truce, the night of prey in the Terminal City—
this tight darkness unknown to both of us.
With a certain fear of their voices' touch
one body calls to the other in this tiring
and calming way of embracing.
Not a single word that stirs, then, the ulcerous air:

separation of their bodies.

And now they are two arduously mutual halves
as in the bright blade of the slicing knife
where the hemispheres of the divided fruit's fresh pulp
contemplate each other without surprise.

WALTER HOEFLER
(1944)

In the habitual process of abandoning the poems he has written and continually reworking them, Walter Hoefler has published virtually nothing. The selection of poems that follows begins with five hermetic texts from *Second Expulsion from Paradise*, written under a pseudonym in October, 1973. Hoefler composed the poem of greater lyrical breadth, "Under Certain Circumstances," after being dismissed from his teaching job at the Universidad Austral in Valdivia due to a series of events that culminated in a politicized student poetry reading in 1978. The perspective on exile from within the country he is about to leave is unique in Chilean poetry. Hoefler is now living in Darmstadt, West Germany.

DEBAJO DE CADA PIEDRA

Debajo de cada piedra
hay quienes nos enseñaron a vivir
o a preparar gustosos nuestra muerte
cuando ya toda vida había acabado.

Debajo de cada palabra
hay un germen letal que se insinúa
y también algún indicio
de que toda vida comienza
todavía.

HAY ALGUIEN

¿Hay alguien que se lamente
de nuestro olvido,
o somos nosotros
los olvidados de siempre,
los que estuvimos a punto?

Clarines o puñados de tierra
sobre nuestras cabezas.

BENEATH EACH STONE

Beneath each stone
are those who taught us to live
or to prepare our deaths with pleasure
after all life had ended.

Beneath each word
lurks a lethal germ
as well as some sign
that all life is still
beginning.

IS THERE ANYONE

Is there anyone who cries
for our oblivion,
or will we
always be the forgotten,
those who almost won?

Bugles and fistfuls of dirt
over our heads.

EL LUGAR QUE HABITAS

Tierra escandida por el agua
que no te guarda rencor.
El único ojo de vidrio del río
está abierto a tu cielo,
donde los insectos posan sus patas
como pequeñas puñaladas.

SOBREVIVIENTE

El amor y las palabras se resienten
y se consumen como todo lo amado.
Escarabajo que hurga entre nuestros dedos.

THE PLACE YOU INHABIT

Land scanned by water
that bears you no hatred.
The single glass eye of the river
is open to your sky,
where insects descend
like small knives.

SURVIVOR

Love and words grow weak
and waste away like all that's loved.
Beetle squeezing between our fingers.

BAJO CIERTAS CIRCUNSTANCIAS

> "Por hebrero deste presente año de
> 1552 poblé la ciudad de Valdivia,
> tienen de comer cient vecinos."
> Pedro de Valdivia, Cartas, XI
>
> "Une même vague par le monde, une
> même vague depuis Troie."
> Saint-John Perse, Amers, IX,1

Me despido de la ciudad.
Deberé alejarme de ella
sin volver jamás la cabeza.
Estatuas de sal decoran el camino.
Sólo muy a la distancia te será permitido recordarla.
Quizás muera en el camino.
Un pequeño túmulo marcará la distancia exacta.
¿Cuánto te habrás alejado?
Pero tú o alguien, alguna vez, te retornará.

Me despido de la ciudad
reconciliándome con la lluvia,
con la niebla que recubre los ríos,
con las doradas espigas del islote.
Sobre los puentes, trampolines del instante,
abrevio toda otra consideración.
Un semáforo en rojo
impide tu retorno,
amarillo es el horizonte.

Me despido de la ciudad.
Pido excusas por arrogarme ese derecho.
Ese derecho me lo da mi nacimiento.
¡Ay de quien ose arrebatarlo!
que todas mis palabras lo condenen.

·   ·   ·   ·   ·   ·   ·   ·   ·   ·

Me despido de la ciudad
recordando el gesto del fundador,
no el índice extendido que muestran los billetes,
sino el sueño pesado del cansancio,
la primera noche, el ruido horrible
de la primera soledad y de la vigilia.
Nadie cruzando sus calles,
sólo su oído pegado a la tierra
y al alcance de la mano, las armas,
mientras el fuego crepita y confirma su presencia.

UNDER CERTAIN CIRCUMSTANCES

> "Por hebrero deste presente año de
> 1552 poblé la ciudad de Valdivia,
> tienen de comer cient vecinos."
> Pedro de Valdivia, *Cartas*, XI

> "Une même vague par le monde, une
> même vague depuis Troie."
> Saint-John Perse, *Amers*, IX, 1

I say goodbye to the city.
I must distance myself from it
without ever looking back.
Statues of salt decorate the road.
Only from very far away will I be allowed to remember it.
Perhaps I'll die on the road.
A small mound will mark the exact distance.
How far will I have gone?
But someone, at some time, will bring me back.

I say goodbye to the city
having made peace with the rain,
the fog that covers the rivers,
the golden spikes of grain on tiny islands.
I cross bridges, trampolines of the present,
and shorten all other considerations.
A red traffic light
stops you from returning.
The horizon is yellow.

I say goodbye to the city.
Allow me to claim that right,
the right that is mine by birth.
Who would dare seize it?
Let all my words condemn him.

.   .   .   .

I say goodbye to the city
remembering the gesture of its founder.
Not the pointing finger on our money,
but the weight of dreams, exhaustion,
the first night, the horrible noise
of the first solitude and keeping watch.
No one crossing the streets,
only his ear pressed against the ground
and his weapons close at hand
while the fire crackled and confirmed his presence.

Me despido de la ciudad.
Nada es pequeño para el que ama,
hasta el deshecho pedruzco que arrastra la corriente
hasta el rostro que pasa y nos inquiere.
Mi boca se cierne para cantar lo fundado
y se retrae en la muda despedida.

Me despido de la ciudad.
Ningún recuerdo especial dejo en ella.
Ya no me esmero por saludar a nadie
o quizás sea que ahora los saludo a todos.
En quien no conozco me preparo
para habitar otros rostros, otras sombras.
Otras ciudades adivino
en esos rostros que desconozco,
pero igual los saludo.

Me despido de la ciudad.
En ella nací.
Ahora corto al parecer todo vínculo.
Estoy seguro ya de que mis huesos no le pertenecerán.
Nada deben ya sus calles a mis ojos somnolientos.
Ya no le cobro ninguna imagen,
ya no cierro mis párpados para verla mejor.
Todo se hace claro como el viento.
Alguien debe haber decido por tí.

Sólo cabe aceptarlo.
Hay frases de consuelo:
¡Será para mejor, te hacen un favor!

Me despido de la ciudad
y ya he llegado a otra
donde no podré repetir con orgullo:
aquí he nacido, aquí moriré.
Es una frase tonta, pero tendré que empezar de nuevo,
empezar por imitar el gesto de un nuevo fundador,
terminar de quemar mis naves,
reservándome el último fósforo.

I say goodbye to the city.
There's nothing too small for the one who loves
even the crumbling rock dragged by the current
even the face that stares as it passes by.
My mouth blossoms to sing its founding
and closes in mute farewell.

I say goodbye to the city.
I leave no special memory behind.
I'm no longer worried about greeting anyone
or maybe now I'm greeting everyone.
I'm preparing myself for those I don't know
to inhabit other faces, other shadows.
I foresee other cities
in those faces I do not know
but I greet them just the same.

I say goodbye to the city.
I was born in her.
Now it seems like I'm cutting all ties.
I'm sure now that my bones will not belong to her.
Her streets owe nothing now to my drowsy eyes.
She no longer repays me with any image.
And I don't have to close my eyes to see her better.
Everything becomes as clear as the wind.
Someone must have decided for you.

All that's left is to accept it.
To console you, people say,
"You'll be better off, they're doing you a favor!"

I say goodbye to the city
and I've already arrived in the other one
where I won't be able to say with pride,
"Here, I was born. Here, I will die."
It's silly to say it, but I'll have to begin again,
begin by imitating a new founder,
finish burning my ships and
save the last match for myself.

Me despido de la ciudad,
de sus precoces genios,
de sus pequeños fariseos.
Mis palabras no saben odiar.
Aún con mis enemigos soy capaz de brindar por el porvenir.
Todavía confío en que nadie es culpable,
ni esos dioses, tan indiferentes.

.   .   .   .

Me despido de la ciudad
y ya avizoro otras murallas,
los rostros solidarios,
las manos amigas que saludan tu llegada,
pero allí sólo podré beber por el pasado,
el porvenir sólo lo veo desde aquí.
Quiera alguien que ese momento sea dispensado.

Me despido de la ciudad.
Unas pocas frases silenciosas,
unas pocas letrillas que nadie leerá.
Me despido casi en secreto,
dejando apenas este legado de palabras.

Me despido de la ciudad.
Me despido de sus muertos que conozco,
me despido de los que medran a la sombra de los muertos,
me despido de los muertos, los vivos de mañana.

Me despido de la ciudad,
ya me queda poco tiempo,
he empacado mis cosas,
mi familia esta también dispuesta.
Espero que mi pasaporte esté completamente en regla,
pero para circular por otras partes sólo requiero de unas pocas palabras,
palabras que siempre me permitirán retornar.

Me despido de la ciudad.
Ya hemos limpiado la casa,
ya hemos entregado las llaves.
-Mira, ahí queda una telaraña.
-No la saques, que al menos ella
tenga un buen recuerdo.

I say goodbye to the city,
to its precocious geniuses,
to its small pharisees.
My words don't know how to hate.
I could even toast the future with my enemies.
I still have faith that no one is guilty—
not even those gods who are so indifferent.

.   .   .   .

I say goodbye to the city
and already I see other walls,
faces and friendly hands
welcoming you in solidarity.
But there, I will only be able to drink to the past.
I can only see the future from here.
Someone hopes that moment will never come.

I say goodbye to the city.
A few silent sentences,
a few little letters that no one will read.
I say goodbye almost in secret,
barely leaving this legacy of words.

I say goodbye to the city.
I say goodbye to its dead that I know.
I say goodbye to those who thrive in the shadow of the dead.
I say goodbye to the dead, tomorrow's living.

I say goodbye to the city.
There's not much time left now.
I've packed my things.
My family is ready, too.
I hope my passport is completely in order,
but to circulate in other parts I only need a few words,
words that will always let me return.

I say goodbye to the city.
We've already cleaned the house
and turned in the keys.
"Look, there's a spider web."
"Leave it there. At least it
might have some fond memories."

"NO PODRÍA CONTAR LA HISTORIA. . ."

No podría contar la historia.
Escribo desde otra orilla de la vida.
Pasan aves refrenando el vuelo,
palpando el aire y la llovizna.
Ya no regresarán.
Otro tiempo empieza al margen del reloj.
Pausado, interior, casi reiterado.
La historia ahora sólo es carne en los pequeños recuerdos,
algún trozo de hueso entre los dientes.
La boca no está para palabras.
Las aves se detienen y dejan de croar las ranas.
En el río los peces prosiguen su labor
agitando el barro del fondo.

ESCRIBIR

Persistir en lo que hacemos,
reserva,
pequeño margen
del oficio tenazmente retenido.
Segunda expulsión del paraíso,
agua desbordando sus lagunas.
Pequeña casa donde nadie habita.

"I WOULDN'T BE ABLE TO TELL THE STORY. . ."

I wouldn't be able to tell the story.
I write from the other shore of life.
Birds stalling in mid-flight,
groping for air and light rain.
They will not return.
Another time begins beyond the clock:
slow, interior, almost reiterated.
History is just the meat on tiny memories,
bits of bone between the teeth.
The mouth isn't fit for words.
The birds halt and the frogs stop croaking.
In the river, the fish go on with their work:
stirring the mud on the bottom.

TO WRITE

To persist in what we do,
reserve,
tiny margin
of the work we will never let go.
Second expulsion from paradise,
overflowing ponds.
Small house where no one lives.

PAZ MOLINA

(1945)

Despite the great island of Gabriela Mistral's poetry, there has not been an abundance of important women poets in Chile. The concerns of that Nobel Prize-winning poet do not seem to speak to the younger generations of women. Ironically, the aggressiveness and centripetal violence in Paz Molina's poetry led one critic to compare her work to that of the epitome of masculinity in Chilean poetry, Pablo de Rokha, author of *"El canto del macho anciano."* It was as if Gabriela Mistral had never written *Desolación* or spoken of "the brutal light of the coming day." For a North American reader, some of the following poetry may recall the psychic abysses navigated by Sylvia Plath and Anne Sexton. Now that her children are older, Paz Molina has been able to devote more time to poetry and published her first book, *Memorias de un pájaro asustado*, in 1982.

TU IRA

Como el relumbrar de un ojo en la oscuridad
que se avecina
siento el augurio de tu ira.
Cae un negro pétalo, una culebra silba
y se corroe mi espíritu entre tus garras.

Soy inocente de la tormenta,
(han jurado los dioses protegerme)
sin embargo, el rayo abre espacios.
Cae mi árbol calcinado.

Te pertenezco
mas fue ajena la piedra del suplicio
y ciego el verdugo.
No. No fueron tus manos conscientes
las que ataron mi cuerpo.

Clemencia.
El abdomen herido,
espero el sereno sobrevenir
de la nada.
El gesto que restañe
los labios que sepulten . . .

El tiempo crece y alarga los adioses.

YOUR ANGER

Like the brilliance of an eye in darkness
getting closer
I sense your foreboding anger.
A black petal falls, a snake hisses
and my spirit corrodes between your claws.

I'm innocent of the storm
(the gods have sworn to protect me)
but still a bolt of lightning opens spaces.
My charred tree falls.

I belong to you
yet the stone of torment
was someone else's and
the executioner blind.
No. Your hands did not tie down
my body on purpose.

Clemency.
With my abdomen cut open
I wait for the serene coming
of nothingness.
The look that stops the flow of blood,
the lips that bury . . .

Time grows and prolongs the goodbyes.

EL LLANTO ES UNA ESPECIE DE ATAÚD

Tu rostro es clara forma
que atestigua
el paso clandestino
del tiempo
(astuto propiciador de fines)
El llanto es una especie
de ataúd.

Una cierta clase de
equivocación.

Una manera de
Catástrofe.

O acaso un acierto
involuntario
de la verdad que se acoje
desnuda
después de una tormenta
inesperada.

Porque en ese fluir de esencia
puede aflorar la piel
desconocida.
El hondo vértigo de sinrazón
que habita la memoria.

Y atestiguar su ofrenda
las formas ignoradas
los perfiles
que se amaron un tiempo
y se perdieron.

THE SCREAM IS A KIND OF COFFIN

The clear form of your face
bears witness
to the clandestine passage
of time,
the one who wins the favor
of all endings.

The scream is a kind
of coffin.

Some sort of
mistake.

Some
catastrophe.

Or perhaps an
involuntary skill—
the truth that slinks in
naked
after an unexpected
storm.

Because in that flowing of essence
the unknown skin
may blossom.
The vertigo
where there is no reason,
where memory lives.

And to bear witness to its offering
the ignored forms
the profiles
that for awhile loved
then lost each other.

ACONTECERES COMO PALACIOS

Augur ridículo:
vierte tu inocencia
en el caudal oscuro que te asusta.

Construye balsas
y separa tu sombra
de ti mismo.

Que no se ahoguen
tus difusos contornos
en oráculos.

Prefabricando
aconteceres
de impreciso axioma

como palacios
donde habitar atónito
de sueños

mientras se acerca
la realidad
nadando hacia tu orilla.

EVENTS LIKE PALACES

Ridiculous dreamer:
pour your innocence
into the dark torrent that scares
you.

Build rafts
and separate your shadow
from yourself.

Don't let your diffuse
limits drown
in oracles.

Prefabricating
events
of imprecise axiom

like palaces—
a place to live astonished
in dreams

while reality
comes closer,
swimming toward your shore.

COSAS DE CIEGOS

Anclado en niebla se ilumina un rostro:
tiempo de madrugadas.
Un antifaz esgrime su eficacia
en el vaivén del planeta.
Consciente de atropello se propone
inaugurar el ritmo,
pronosticar el sol,
descabezar al gigante
que suele amedrentar a las princesas.

Cuida de prolongar su epifanía
hacia el borde del instinto.
Manto de soledad que presupone
vestigios de coraje.
Cose su desnudez una promesa,
aguja de cristal entre los labios.

Abuela del ayer trae sonidos
como armarios
donde hubiera dormido la esperanza.

Su soledad impone alondras
que bordan en el cielo
la inocencia de las nubes.

THINGS OF THE BLIND

A face shines, anchored in fog:
season of rising suns.
A mask wields its powers
in the planet's coming and going.
At the risk of being crushed, it decides
to establish its own rhythm,
divine the sun,
cut off the head of the giant
who is used to frightening princesses.

Carefully, it extends the epiphany
toward the edge of instinct.
Shawl of solitude presupposing
the last traces of courage.
A promise sews up its nakedness,
crystal needle through lips.

Yesterday's grandmother brings sounds
like closets
where hope would have slept.

Her solitude imposes larks
that embroider
the innocence of clouds in the sky.

Despacito por las piedras.
Que no te asuste el grito verde
de los entusiastas.

No vayas a creer demasiado
en tu propia fábula.

Acaso sea bueno que te aquietes
y midas, con prudencia, la distancia.

Porque el espacio que has de salvar
es ancho, como el tiempo.

Y los ratones no tenemos alas.

Go slowly over the stones.
Don't let the green scream
of the enthusiasts scare you.

Don't believe too much
in your own fable.

It might be a good idea to calm down
and carefully measure the distance.

Because the space you will cross
is wide like time.

And we mice don't have wings.

GONZALO MILLÁN

(1947)

The short, ornate poems of Gonzalo Millán's first book, *Relación personal*, spin on the axis of adolescence. During the next ten years, from 1968-78, Millán's language underwent an increasing objectivization due, in part, to his reading of poets such as William Carlos Williams, Reznikoff, Zukofsky, Oppen and Rakosi. The poet's second book, *La ciudad*, is a work of 68 numbered texts with a narrative structure and a relentless reiterative power in which historical time unfolds in an urban space. Individual poems are woven together in *La ciudad* through the repetition of key verbs and nouns that continually take on new meanings in their different contexts. The erasing of the conventional lyrical voice and the insistent realism of the long poem have caused critics to dismiss it as monotonous and excessive. Others have praised Millán's capacity to create a true poetic universe with its own laws. Gonzalo Millán left Chile in 1974 and presently resides in Canada.

TOCO RONDAS INFANTILES
CON UNA MUECA EN LOS LABIOS

Un muñeco podrido bajo tierra en un jardín
y las ciruelas perdiendo el gusto ácido en el agua.
Tras las carcomidas lanzas de madera de una reja
se le pegan los pétalos en los labios
a un niño que muerde flores rojas.
Y yo con mis grandes manos, desde lejos,
comienzo a tocar el piano de juguete.

LOS AROS DE HIERRO DEL TRICICLO
SIN GOMAS Y EL RASCAR DE UN CLAVO

Caemos de pronto del amor
y somos dos migas sucias
flotando en un platillo con agua
o la mosca sin alas
que el dedo hace correr sobre la mesa.

Yo retiro tu viejo cabello
enrollado en mi oreja
y hacemos vibrar
la gillette del odio en nuestras bocas
hasta que el hedor de verdes aguas de floreros
nos hace soltar la arena
que tenían las manos para lanzarnos a los ojos
y abrir de nuevo las ventanas.

I PLAY CHILDISH SONGS WITH A GRIMACE ON MY LIPS

A rotten doll buried in a garden
and the plums in water losing their sharp taste.
Behind the gnawed away wooden spears of a fence
petals stick to the lips
of a child chewing red flowers.
And from far away, with my huge hands,
I begin to play the toy piano.

THE IRON WHEELS OF THE TRICYCLE WITHOUT TIRES AND A SCRAPING NAIL

Suddenly we fall from love
and we're two dirty crumbs
floating in a saucer of water
or the wingless fly
flicked by a finger across the table.

I remove your old hair
wrapped around my ear
and we shake
the razor of hatred in our mouths
until the green water's stench in vases
makes us release the sand
we kept in our hands to throw in each other's
eyes
and open the windows once again.

RINCÓN

Una antigua tira de boletos
de una feria de entretenciones,
la huincha de trapo para medir.

Y una luna roja de otro planeta,
la pelota de goma de un niño
que rodó, quieta, a un rincón.

NADIE

Las calles están silenciosas
y desiertas. Solamente cruzan
las sombras de los árboles.

No se oyen pájaros, bocinas
ni siquiera el motor inminente
de un auto siempre aproximándose.

Los ascensores, las escaleras
y pasillos de los edificios, vacíos.

En una cocina un charco
en torno al refrigerador
que se deshiela
y la puerta abierta.

Conservada en el hielo
no hay más que una arveja
muy pequeña, redonda y verde.

CORNER

An old roll of tickets
from an amusement park,
the tape measure.

And a red moon from another planet:
a child's rubber ball
that rolled quietly into a corner.

NO ONE

The streets, silent
and deserted, are crossed
only by the shadows of trees.

No birds can be heard, no horns,
not even the imminent engine
of an approaching car.

The elevators, stairways
and corridors in buildings: empty.

In a kitchen a puddle
below a defrosting
refrigerator
with its naked shelves
and open door.

Preserved in ice
there's nothing more than a pea—
very small, round and green.

POEMA *13* DE LA CIUDAD

Llueve.
La lluvia mancha las calles.
El asfalto mojado es lustroso.
Los peatones se cubren.
El; sombrero cubre la cabeza.
El paraguas resguarda de la lluvia.
Los zapatos entran en las galochas.
Las galochas son de goma.
La pelota rebota en el suelo.
La lluvia rebota en el suelo.
Llueve a cántaros.
Los cántaros son de barro.
La lluvia forma charcos.
En los charcos se forma barro.
La lluvia forma burbujas al caer en los charcos.
Los autos salpican.
El agua rebota en el techo.
Los techos se llueven.
Las goteras caen en tarros.
Las aguas corren por los tejados.
Los canalones recogen las aguas.
Los techos chorrean.
La lluvia golpea las ventanas.
Las gotas resbalan por los vidrios.
La lluvia moja.
La lluvia humedece las paredes.
La tierra se empapa.
Llueve en la ciudad.
Llueve en el poema.
El anciano escribe.
Las gotas de lluvia no son centavos.
Ojalá fueran centavos las gotas de lluvia.

POEM 13 FROM *THE CITY*

It's raining.
The rain stains the streets.
The wet asphalt shines.
The pedestrians cover themselves.
The hat covers the head.
The umbrella gives protection from the rain.
Shoes step into galoshes.
The galoshes are made of rubber.
The ball is made of rubber.
The ball bounces on the ground.
The rain bounces on the ground.
It's raining buckets.
Buckets made of mud.
The rain forms puddles.
Mud forms in the puddles.
The rain forms bubbles when it falls in puddles.
The cars splash water.
Water bounces on rooftops.
Rooftops rain on each other.
The drops fall into buckets.
Water flows over shingles.
Gutters fill with water.
Rooftops drip.
Rain strikes windows.
The drops slide down the glass.
The rain gets things wet.
The rain runs down the walls.
The earth is soaked.
It's raining in the city.
It's raining in the poem.
The old man is writing.
The drops of rain aren't coins.
If only the drops of rain were coins.

POEMA *20* DE LA CIUDAD

Cae una lluvia torrencial.
La lluvia hincha los torrentes.
Los torrentes causan inundaciones.
Hoy función
A beneficio de los inundados.
Las lluvias son indispensables para la agricultura.
Las lluvias fecundan la tierra.
El trigo germina por primavera.
Las espigas de trigo contienen granos.
El arado se enredó en las raíces.
Los bueyes se acoplan al arado.
El campesino picanea los bueyes.
Escasea el trigo este año.
El paso de la tropa estropeó las siembras.
Los ratones hacen estragos en los graneros.
Las malezas esquilman los campos.
Escasea el dinero.
Tengo un puñado escaso de harina.
Encarece el pan.
Vivimos con escasez.
Está escasa la comida.
El trabajo escasea.
Los cesantes abundan.
El aceite escasea.
Abunda el agua.
El aceite es más espeso que el agua.
El aceite se hiela cuando hace frío.
El aceite penetra las telas.
La espada penetra las carnes.
La espada termina en punta.

POEM 20 FROM *THE CITY*

A torrential rain falls.
The rain swells the torrents.
The torrents cause floods.
Today, a benefit
for all the inundated people.
The rains are indispensable for agriculture.
The rains fertilize the earth.
The wheat germinates by spring.
The spikes of wheat contain grains.
The plow was tangled in the roots.
The oxen are hitched up to the plow.
The *campesino* prods the oxen.
Wheat is scarce this year.
Troops trampled the sown fields.
Mice ruin the granaries.
Weeds exhaust the fields.
Money is scarce.
I have scarcely a handful of flour.
Bread is getting expensive.
We live with scarcity.
Food is scarce.
Work is getting scarcer.
The unemployed are abundant.
Oil is getting scarce.
Water is abundant.
Oil is thicker than water.
Oil freezes when it gets cold.
Oil penetrates cloth.
The sword penetrates flesh.
The sword ends in a point.

POEMA *48* DE LA CIUDAD

El río invierte el curso de su corriente.
El agua de las cascadas sube.
La gente empieza a caminar retrocediendo.
Los caballos caminan hacia atrás.
Los militares deshacen lo desfilado.
Las balas salen de las carnes.
Las balas entran en los cañones.
Los oficiales enfundan sus pistolas.
La corriente se devuelve por los cables.
La corriente penetra por los enchufes.
Los torturados dejan de agitarse.
Los torturados cierran sus bocas.
Los campos de concentración se vacían.
Aparecen los desaparecidos.
Los muertos salen de sus tumbas.
Los aviones vuelan hacia atrás.
Los "rockets" suben hacia los aviones.
Allende dispara.
Las llamas se apagan.
Se saca el casco.
La Moneda se reconstituye íntegra.
Su cráneo se recompone.
Sale a un balcón.
Allende retrocede hasta Tomás Moro.
Los detenidos salen de espalda de los estadios.
11 de Septiembre.
Regresan aviones con refugiados.
Chile es un país democrático.
Las fuerzas armadas respetan la constitución.
Los militares vuelven a sus cuarteles.
Renace Neruda.
Vuelve en una ambulancia a Isla Negra.
Le duele la próstata. Escribe.
Víctor Jara toca la guitarra. Canta.
Los discursos entran en las bocas.
El tirano abraza a Prat.
Desaparece. Prat revive.
Los cesantes son recontratados.
Los obreros desfilan cantando
¡Venceremos!

POEM 48 FROM *THE CITY*

The river reverses its flow.
Waterfalls rise.
People begin to recede.
Horses trot backwards.
Soldiers break ranks.
Bullets leave the flesh.
Bullets enter the gunbarrels.
Officers put away their pistols.
The current flows out through the cords.
The current penetrates the outlets.
Those who were being tortured stop shaking.
Those who were being tortured close their mouths.
The concentration camps are emptied.
Those who were missing appear.
The dead rise from their graves.
The planes fly backwards.
The rockets climb toward the planes.
Allende fires his gun.
The flames die down.
He takes off his helmet.
La Moneda makes itself whole again.
His skull mends itself.
He steps onto a balcony.
Allende goes back to Tomás Moro Street.
Those who were arrested leave the stadiums backwards.
September 11.
Planes full of refugees return.
Chile is a democratic country.
The armed forces respect the constitution.
The soldiers return to their barracks.
Neruda is reborn.
He returns to Isla Negra by ambulance.
His prostate is painful. He writes.
Victor Jara plays the guitar. He sings.
Speeches enter mouths.
The tyrant embraces Prat.
He disappears. Prat lives again.
The unemployed are rehired.
The workers are marching, singing
Venceremos!

POEMA *60* DE LA CIUDAD

El anciano se mira al espejo.
El espejo repite las imágenes.
El poema es un espejo.
Mi hermano está en el lado contrario.
Nos vestían iguales.
Yo soy contrario al gobierno.
Los hermanos no se avienen.
Uno dice blanco.
El otro dice negro.
Uno dice rojo.
El otro dice negro.

La tinta es negra.
El papel es blanco.
El anciano manuscribe.
Arruga una hoja de papel.
El anciano tiene la piel arrugada.
Los miopes usan lentes.
El anciano usa lentes.
El anciano tiene la salud quebrantada.
El anciano corrige.
La goma borra lo escrito.
Donde había un edificio deja un sitio baldío.
Un cambio de sintaxis invierte el curso del río.
Un punto detiene la ciudad.
La tierra está inmóvil en el espacio.
El mar está inmóvil.
No pasa el tiempo.
Nada se mueve.
Los habitantes están paralizados.
Reina la inmovilidad.
Cae una nieve invisible.
Sólo los dedos del anciano se mueven.
El anciano relee.

POEM 60 FROM *THE CITY*

The old man looks at himself in the mirror.
The mirror repeats images.
The poem is a mirror.
Twins are identical.
My brother is on the other side.
We dress the same.
I am against the government.
The brothers don't agree.
One says white.
The other says black.
One says red.
The other says black.

Ink is black.
Paper is white.
The old man writes in longhand.
He crumples a piece of paper.
The old man has wrinkled skin.
The nearsighted use glasses.
The old man uses glasses.
The old man is in deteriorating health.
The old man corrects.
The eraser erases what's written.
Where there was a building he leaves a razed site.
A change of syntax changes the course of the river.
A period stops the city.
The earth is immobile in space.
The sea is immobile.
Time does not pass.
Nothing moves.
The inhabitants are paralyzed.
Immobility reigns.
An invisible snow falls.
Only the old man's fingers move.
The old man rereads.

Los dedos del anciano recorren las letras.
El anciano encuentra el nombre del tirano.
El anciano borra su nombre.
Su nombre no merece ser recordado.
El anciano encuentra los nombres de los asesinos.
El anciano borra los nombres de los asesinos.
Sus nombres no se olvidarán.
A su hora recibirán castigo.

VISIÓN

Y después de ir
con los ojos cerrados
por la oscuridad que nos lleva
abrir los ojos y ver
la oscuridad que nos lleva
con los ojos abiertos
y cerrar los ojos.

The old man's fingers follow the letters.
The old man finds the name of the tyrant.
The old man erases his name.
His name doesn't deserve to be remembered.
The old man finds the names of the murderers.
The old man erases the names of the murderers.
Their names will not be forgotten.
In due time they will be punished.

VISION

And after going
with our eyes closed
through the darkness
that carries us
opening our eyes and seeing
the darkness that carries us
with our eyes open
and closing our eyes.

JUAN CAMERON

(1947)

Juan Cameron's poetry is a corrosive blend of irony and black humor that often ridicules the institutions and habits of the upper class. A section of his book, *Perro de circo (Circus Dog)*, which won the Rudyard Kipling Prize in 1978, is a compendium of diseases, a pathology of the human condition in Chile after the military coup. Other poems seem written on the run while the poet hides in a cheap hotel, makes do on some remote farm in the countryside, or drives a truck in exile down the highways of Argentina. At the end of the 1960s and into the 1970s, Cameron collaborated with the writers of the Café Cinema in Viña del Mar that included Juan Luis Martínez and Raúl Zurita. Cameron's wanderings led him back to Valparaíso where he lives with his family in a house that overlooks the bay of the port and is only a few steep blocks from where he was born and lived as a boy. In 1982, Cameron won the prestigious Gabriela Mistral Poetry Prize.

LA HORA SEÑALADA

Está bien   el paraíso lo perdimos por precario
comodato de ángel guardián   era la hora
desolojados fuimos a lanzazos   a besos
mejor dicho he armas   (no quiero herir a nadie)
Nos han vedado el cielo   ya el infierno
Es el limbo   estamos donde estábamos
nos cobijan qqui   es la verdad
pero eso es todo
Ahora que vagamos en busca de la luna
oscura está la gleba   los caminos
marchan sobre sí mismos   era la hora
La hora señalada se dispara en la sien
Sólo puertas mentales se nos abren ahora.

PRETÉRITO
IMPERFECTO

La lluvia llega a contemplar la plaza
Las hojas   marchitas consignas del verano
que pronto tornará

De nada me arrepiento
Volverá la telaraña después de la tormenta
No es tiempo de metáforas

Mi pequeña patria   el sistema solar
me basta
Mi insignificancia es infinita

La campana de la escuela
*   suena en este vaso*
En él giran los astros como años perdidos
De nada me arrepiento
*   Afuera   llueve.*

THE SIGNALLED HOUR

Fine   so we lost paradise because
of some guardian angel's broken lease   it was time
We were evicted at spear-point   nudged out
at gunpoint I mean   (I don't want to hurt anyone)
They've banned heaven   and hell too
It's limbo   we're right where we were
they give us shelter   it's true
but that's all it is
Now that we wander in search of the moon
the plowed earth is dark   the roads
walk down themselves   it was time
The signalled hour shoots itself in the head
Only doors of the mind open for us now.

IMPERFECT
PRETERITE

The rain arrives to contemplate the plaza
The leaves   withered slogans of the summer
that will soon return

I don't regret anything
The spider web will be back after the storm
This isn't the time for metaphors

My tiny country   the solar system
it's enough for me
My insignificance is infinite

The school bell
                    rings in this glass
where the stars spin like lost years
I don't regret anything
                    Outside   it's raining.

CUANDO SE ACABE

Aún no podemos anunciar nuestra partida
Hemos perdido los pasos del mañana
Ciertas imágenes de la infancia
(meras justificaciones)
nos acompañan al último fuego de esta casa

Cuando se acabe el kerosene estaremos lejos
El humo negro de la estufa describirá círculos en las paredes
buscándonos en las manchas de la lluvia
como un general busca en un mapa

Cuando se acabe el fuego no quedarán trazos de las complicaciones
Antiguos gestos crepitarán en las cenizas
La rueca su estambre ya habrá adormecido
como los relojes
como los teléfonos
como fotografías de otro tiempo

Cuando se acabe el día los recuerdos
serán rehenes de otra tierra.

WHEN IT'S OVER

We still can't announce when we'll leave
We've lost the future's trail
Certain images from our youth
(mere justifications)
come with us to the last fire
we'll light in this house

When the kerosene runs out we'll be far away
The stove's black smoke will mark circles
on the walls stained with rain
looking for us
the way a general pores over a map

When the fire dies down the remains
of our dilemma will be gone
Old gestures will smolder in the ash
The spindle and its wool will fall asleep
like the clocks
like the telephones
like photographs from another time

When the day is over our memories
will be the hostages of another land

HERÁCLITO

Si regreso a tu arroyo
ya no seré el mismo ni sus aguas
bañarán mi cuerpo de la ausencia
Tu casa estará desierta
como los perros en sus huesos
querrán mover las colas que les faltan.

RUTA SIETE

En el lejano oeste de los sueños
en el free way del pensamiento
de la ira
retornamos gachas las cabezas
escupiendo el sol.

HERACLITUS

If I return to your stream
it won't be the same anymore
nor will its waters cleanse
the absence from my body
The rooms of your house
will be deserted
like the skeletons of dogs
who want to wag tails
they do not have.

ROUTE SEVEN

In the far west of dreams
on the freeway of thought
of rage
we return slumped forward
spitting the sun.

SUBWAY

Padre   no leas a Shakespeare
hay estatuas en el Metro   la Pietá
sostiene los huesos del suicida
La telenovela no es Hamlet
ni los somnolientos pasos
tremolan la Venus metropolitana
bajo las venas metropolitanas

Padre   es tarde en Chile
la lluvia cruza el mundo como fantasma
la cultura son rieles   los ángeles
tronan las trompetas en los túneles
azules del ocaso   es tarde   es tarde
la inflación ha causado demasiadas bajas en la
tierra de nadie
& yo te lanzo frases
misiles u oraciones después de los ataques
una columna de fantasmas mis palabras
ladridos en ladrillos se deslizan
bajo el neón vernacular

Padre   no leas a Shakespeare
alza tus ojos a los ángeles ateridos de tedio
ángeles subterraneos liberados de pájaros & flores
esperando la daga celestial   la paloma
descendida a la tierra precaria   a la oscura
en el sube & baja de las escaleras mecánicas

Padre   en cuál estación
*   en cuál tren*
*   dónde?*
Las estatuas son ángeles   caminan   salen de las cloacas
*   bailan*
arriba hay un mundo   dicen

SUBWAY

Father   don't read Shakespeare
there are statues in the Metro   the Pietà
holds the suicide's bones
The soap opera isn't Hamlet
nor do the drowsy footsteps
shake the metropolitan Venus
under the metropolitan veins

Father   it's late in Chile
rain crosses the world like a ghost
culture is the train tracks   angels
blast their trumpets in the blue tunnels
at dusk   it's late   it's late
inflation has meant too many casualties
in no man's land
& I launch sentences toward you
missiles or prayers after the attacks
a column of ghosts   my words
howling over the bricks
under the neon vernacular

Father   don't read Shakespeare
lift your eyes to the angels frozen in boredom
subterranean angels free of birds & flowers
waiting for the celestial dagger   the dove
that came down to this precarious land
in darkness   up and down the escalators

Father   in which station
            on which train
                    where?
The statues are angels   walking   coming up from the sewers
                    dancing
there's a world up there   they say

Padre   alza tu vista
súbeme en tus párpados   besa esta frente
Es tarde en Chile
                es tarde
Quiero ver los días anteriores
quiero la sal del aire alcanzarla
Padre
        ya no leas a Shakespeare
Es mía la calavera sobre tu mano
& el último tren atraviesa tus ojos.

PLAYA*

Una piedra feliz nortea la bahía
al sur en la imagen del ausente
según dice la letra que leemos a oscuras.
Desde aquí se ve el mundo
los puertos encallados más allá de las nubes
los pueblos donde parlan de la perdida Itaca
donde a nadie despierta este organillo
instalado en la arena
Mas el sur no es el sur sino el este
el norweste acusando a los vientos
& el gallo en la veleta un petrolero
& la esperanza un container abierto por pandora
& la piedra feliz   es sólo eso
una roca apuntando hacia el vacío
crecido junto a ustedes.

---

*Piedra Feliz es una roca ubicada en la playa de las Torpederas en
Valparaíso. Allí el mar es bravo y la gente usa la roca para suicidarse.

Father   lift your eyes
pick me up with your eyelids   kiss this forehead
It's late in Chile
                        it's late
I want to see the days gone by
I want the salt in the air
I want to touch it
Father
        don't read Shakespeare any more
the skull in your hand is mine
& the last train passes through your eyes

BEACH

A happy stone* juts north of the bay
but south in the song by someone
who isn't here with us in the dark.
From here you can see the world:
the ports running aground beyond the clouds,
the towns where people talk about the lost Ithaca
where this organ grinder playing
music on the sand wakes no one.
But south isn't south. It's east
the northwest accusing the winds
& the rooster on the weathervane is an oil tanker
& hope is a box opened by Pandora
& the happy stone is just that
a rock pointing toward the emptiness
that rose around all of you.

---

*Piedra Feliz is a rock located on Torpederas Beach in Valparaíso. The sea is
rough there and people use the rock to commit suicide.

RAÚL ZURITA

(1951)

New Chilean poetry is being measured in terms of Raúl Zurita. The limited outlets for literary criticism in Chile are filled with his presence—a phenomenon that could be considered a disproportionate highlighting of the poet's obvious talent. Some critics have portrayed Zurita's corporal acts of self-aggression and "exhibitionism" as sensationalist and scandalous. Others have located the acts in their artistic and historical contexts and hailed Zurita as a proponent of a new *vanguardia*. The controversy notwithstanding, Zurita's two published books have given him an important place in the formidable poetic tradition in Chile.

In *Purgatorio*, there is a preoccupation with the self that results in its successive multiplication, deification and atomization: the poet becomes various doubles not confined to the masculine sex, an omniscient prophet in the desert, and an electroencephalographic study. While it may be true that technical concerns have superceded social concerns in Zurita's poetry, it would be misguided to categorize the work as ahistorical. One of Zurita's poetic recourses, for example, is the political allegory in "The Cordilleras of *Il Duce*." The trajectory in Zurita's work moves from the universe that revolves around the individual in *Purgatorio* toward the collective aspirations of a country and a continent in *Anteparaíso*. The Biblical sources and language that form an integral part of both works reflect, to a certain extent, the Messianic, mystical impulse of Christianity in Chile that has replaced the dogmatic ideologies of political parties that became illegal after September, 1973.

Zurita's studies to become a civil engineer manifest themselves in the innovative symmetric structures of his books and a mathematical obsession with order. In the early seventies, Zurita collaborated with Juan Luis Martínez and other writers associated with the Café Cinema in Viña del Mar. In 1979, Zurita, along with his wife, Diamela Eltit, and others formed the group called C.A.D.A. (*Colectivos de Acciones de Arte*).

The following selection of poems is an attempt to extract a geographic unity from Zurita's published work. The poet internalizes the desert, the beaches and the mountains of Chile so that they become a spiritual, human landscape.

LA VIDA NUEVA

Continuando con un itinerario previamente trazado, el 2 de junio de 1982 Raúl Zurita realizó sobre la ciudad de Nueva York el poema "La Vida Nueva," escrito en el cielo. Cada una de las frases de este poema, ejecutadas mediante aviones, midió entre 7 y 9 kms. de largo y sus fotografías se incluyen en el libro Anteparaíso. *Lo que sigue es el texto del poema:*

> MI DIOS ES HAMBRE
> MI DIOS ES NIEVE
> MI DIOS ES NO
> MI DIOS ES DESENGAÑO
> MI DIOS ES CARROÑA
> MI DIOS ES PARAISO
> MI DIOS ES PAMPA
> MI DIOS ES CHICANO
> MI DIOS ES CANCER
> MI DIOS ES VACIO
> MI DIOS ES HERIDA
> MI DIOS ES GHETTO
> MI DIOS ES DOLOR
> MI DIOS ES
> MI AMOR DE DIOS

"El poema fue escrito sobre el cielo en idioma español por ser mi lengua materna pero sobre todo como un homenaje a los grupos minoritarios de todas partes del mundo, representados en este caso por la población hispano-parlante de los Estados Unidos.

"Cuando diseñé este proyecto yo pensé que el cielo era precisamente el lugar hacia el cual todas las comunidades han dirigido sus miradas porque han creído ver allí las señas de sus destinos y que entonces, la más gran ambición a la que se podría aspirar es tener ese mismo cielo como página donde cualquiera pudiese escribir. Al pensarlo también recordé una frase de San Juan que decía: 'Vuestros nombres están grabados en el cielo.'

"Poemas escritos en el cielo como el Juicio Final de Miguel Angel en la cúpula de San Pedro. Eso pensé y me acordé de mi padre."

Raúl Zurita

THE NEW LIFE

Continuing with a previously planned itinerary, on June 2, 1982
Raúl Zurita wrote the poem, "The New Life," in the sky over New
York. Each one of the sentences of this poem, executed by means of
airplanes, measured between 7 and 9 kms. in length. Photographs of
this poem are included in the book, *Anteparaíso*. What follows is the
text of the poem:

MY GOD IS HUNGER
MY GOD IS SNOW
MY GOD IS NO
MY GOD IS DISILLUSION
MY GOD IS CARRION
MY GOD IS PARADISE
MY GOD IS PAMPA
MY GOD IS CHICANO
MY GOD IS CANCER
MY GOD IS EMPTINESS
MY GOD IS WOUND
MY GOD IS GHETTO
MY GOD IS PAIN
MY GOD IS
MY LOVE OF GOD

"The poem was written in the sky in Spanish because it is my mother
tongue but above all as a homage to minorities all over the world,
represented in this case by the Spanish-speaking population of the
United States.

"When I designed this project I thought that the sky was precisely the
place toward which all communities lifted their eyes in their belief
that the signs of their fate could be seen there. So, the greatest
aspiration a person could have would be to use the sky itself as a page
where anyone could write. Thinking about this, I also remember
something that Saint John said: 'Your names are engraved in the
sky.'

"Poems written in the sky like Michelangelo's "Last Judgment" on
Saint Peter's Dome. That's what I thought and I remembered my
father."

Raúl Zurita

COMO UN SUEÑO

*Mira qué cosa: el Desierto de
Atacama son puras manchas
sabías? claro   pero no te
costaba nada mirarte un poco
también a ti mismo y decir:
Anda yo también soy una buena
mancha Cristo -oye lindo no
has visto tus pecados? bien
pero entonces déjalo mejor
encumbrarse por esos cielos
manchado   como en tus sueños*

*COMO ESPEJISMOS Y AURAS EL INRI ES MI MENTE
EL DESIERTO DE CHILE*

LIKE A DREAM

Hey look at that: the Atacama
Desert   it's just stains
you know?   sure   but it
wouldn't have been so hard
for you to take a little look
at yourself too and say:
Hey   I'm a good stain
too Christ—listen pretty boy
haven't you seen your sins?   okay
but it would be better then
to let it rise through those skies
stained   like in your dreams

LIKE MIRAGES AND AURAS THE INRI IS MY MIND
THE DESERT OF CHILE

I

A LAS INMACULADAS LLANURAS

i. *Dejemos pasar el infinito del Desierto de Atacama*

ii. *Dejemos pasar la esterilidad de estos desiertos*

Para que desde las piernas abiertas de mi madre se levante una Plegaria que se cruce con el infinito del Desierto de Atacama y mi madre no sea entonces sino un punto de encuentro en el camino

iii. *Yo mismo seré entonces una Plegaria encontrada en el camino*

iv. *Yo mismo seré las piernas abiertas de mi madre*

Para que cuando vean alzarse ante sus ojos los desolados paisajes del Desierto de Atacama mi madre se concentre en gotas de agua y sea la primera lluvia en el desierto

v. *Entonces veremos aparecer el Infinito del Desierto*

iv. *Dado vuelta desde sí mismo hasta dar con las piernas de mi madre*

vii. *Entonces sobre el vacío del mundo se abrirá completamente el verdor infinito del Desierto de Atacama*

I

TO THE IMMACULATE PLAINS

i.   Let's allow the infinity of the Atacama Desert to pass

ii. Let's allow the sterility of these deserts to pass

      So that from my mother's parted legs a prayer rises to
      intersect the infinity of the Atacama Desert and my mother
      then is nothing but a meeting point on the road

iii. I too will be a Prayer then encountered on the road

iv. I too will be the parted legs of my mother

So that when you see the desolate landscape of the Atacama Desert
rise before your eyes my mother condenses into drops of water and is
the first rain in the desert

v.   Then we will see the Infinity of the Desert appear

vi. Turning itself inside out until it finds my mother's legs

vii. Then opening its entirety over the world's emptiness
     the infinite greenness of the Atacama Desert

LAS ESPEJEANTES PLAYAS

i.   *Las playas de Chile no fueron más que un apodo para
      las innombradas playas de Chile*

ii.   *Chile entero no fue más que un apodo frente a las costas
      que entonces se llamaron playas innombradas de Chile*

iii. *Bautizados hasta los sin nombres se hicieron allí un
      santoral sobre estas playas que recién entonces pudieron
      ser las innombradas costas de la patria*

*En que Chile no fue el nombre de las playas de Chile sino sólo unos
apodos mojando esas riberas para que incluso los roqueríos fueran el
bautizo que les llamó playa a nuestros hijos*

iv.   *Nuestros hijos fueron entonces un apodo rompiéndose
      entre los roqueríos*

v.   *Bautizados ellos mismos fueron los santorales de
      estas costas*

vi.   *Todos los sin nombre fueron así los amorosos hijos de
      la patria*

*En que los hijos de Chile no fueron los amorosos hijos de Chile sino
un santoral revivido entre los roqueríos para que nombrados ellos
mismos fuesen allí el padre que les clamaron tantos hijos*

vii. *Porque nosotros fuimos el padre que Chile nombró en
      los roqueríos*

viii. *Chile fue allí el amor por el que clamaban en sus gritos*

ix.   *Entonces Chile entero fue el sueño que apodaron en la
      playa aurado esplendente por todos estos vientos
      gritándoles la bautizada bendita que soñaron*

THE RADIANT BEACHES

i.   The beaches of Chile were nothing more than a nickname for the unnamed beaches of Chile

ii. All of Chile was nothing more than a nickname before the coasts which then were called unnamed beaches of Chile

iii. Baptized even those without names made themselves a calendar of saints there upon these beaches that just then could be the unnamed coasts of the motherland

In that Chile was not the name of the beaches of Chile but only some nicknames washing over those shores so that even the rocks were the baptism that gave our children the name beach

iv. Our children were then a nickname crashing among the rocks

v.   Baptized they themselves were the calendars of saints of these coasts

vi. All of those without a name were thus the lovely children of the motherland

In that the children of Chile were not the lovely children of Chile but a calendar of saints revived among the rocks so that once named there they as so many children were the father they called to themselves

vii. Because we were the father that Chile named upon the rocks

viii. Chile there was the love they cried for

ix.   Then all of Chile that they nicknamed on the beach was the dream   with its aura   splendorous   into these winds screaming at all the blessed baptized who they dreamed

LAS PLAYAS DE CHILE X

*Yo lo vi soltando los remos acurrucarse
contra el fondo del bote La playa aún se
espejeaba en la opaca luz de sus ojos*

*La playa aún se espejeaba en sus ojos pero apenas como un territorio
irreal opacándoles la mirada alargado evanescente en un nuevo
Chile mojándoles las costas que creyeron*

   *i.   Hecho un ánima sintió como se le iban soltando los
         remos de las manos*

  *ii.   Empapado   toda la vida se le fue desprendiendo como
         si ella misma fuera los remos que se le iban yendo de
         entre los dedos*

 *iii.   Incluso su propio aliento le sonó ajeno mientras se
         dejaba caer de lado   suavemente   como un copo de
         nieve   contra las frágiles tablas que hasta allí lo
         llevaron*

*En que la playa nunca volvería a espejearse en sus ojos sino acaso el
relumbrar de un nuevo mundo que les fuera adhiriendo otra luz en
sus pupilas empañadas erráticas alzándoles de frente el horizonte
que les arrasó de lágrimas la cara*

  iv.   Porque sólo allí la playa espejeó en sus ojos

   *v.   Recién entonces pudo sentir sobre sus mejillas el aire
         silbante de esas costas*

  *vi.   Unicamente allí pudo llorar sin contenerse por esa
         playa que volvía a humedecerle la mirada*

*Porque la playa nunca espejearía en sus ojos sino mejor en el
derramarse de todas las utopías como un llanto incontenible que se le
fuera desprendiendo del pecho hirviente desgarrado despejando la
costa que Chile entero le vio adorarse en la iluminada de estos sueños*

THE BEACHES OF CHILE X

I saw him dropping the oars   crouch
in the bottom of the boat   The beach still
shone in the opaque light of his eyes

The beach still shone in his eyes but just barely like an unreal
territory   blinding them   extended   evanescent   in a new Chile
washing over the coasts that believed

    i.   Turned into a spirit he felt how the oars were slipping
        from his hands

    ii.   Drenched his entire life drifted away from him as if it
        were the oars falling from his fingers

    iii.   Even his own breath sounded foreign to him as he let
        himself fall to one side gently like a snowflake against
        the fragile boards that had carried him that far

In that the beach would never shine again in his eyes but perhaps the
radiance of a new world fusing another light to his pupils   tarnished
pilgrims lifting them toward the horizon that brought forth tears to
cover his face

    iv   Because only there did the beach shine in his eyes

    v.   Just then could he feel on his cheeks the whistling air of
        those coasts

    vi.   There and only there could he cry without constraint
        along that beach where his vision was awash once more

Because the beach would shine not in his eyes but in the overflowing
of all the utopias like a scream that can't be contained breaking free
from his chest   boiling   torn loose   sweeping the coast that all of
Chile saw him adore in the brilliance of these dreams

LAS UTOPÍAS

i. *Todo el desierto pudo ser Notre-Dame pero fue el
    desierto de Chile*

ii. *Todas las playas pudieron ser Chartres pero sólo
     fueron las playas de Chile*

iii. *Chile entero pudo ser Nuestra Señora de Santiago pero
      áridos estos paisajes no fueron sino los evanescentes
      paisajes chilenos*

*Donde los habitantes de Chile pudieron no ser los habitantes de Chile
sino un Ruego que les fuera ascendiendo hasta copar el cielo que
miraron   dulces   ruborosos   transparentándose como si nadie los
hubiera fijado en sus miradas*

iv. *Porque el cielo pudo no ser el cielo sino ellos mismos
     celestes cubriendo como si nada los áridos paisajes que
     veían*

v. *Esos habrían sido así los dulces habitantes de Chile
    silenciosos   agachados   poblándo las capillas de su
    Ruego*

vi. *Ellos mismos podrían haber sido entonces las pobladas
     capillas de Chile*

*Donde Chile   pudo no ser el paisaje de Chile pero sí el cielo azul que
miraron y los paisajes habrían sido entonces un Ruego sin fin que se
les escapa de los labios   largo   como un soplo   de toda la patria
haciendo un amor que les poblara las alturas*

vii. *Chile será entonces un amor poblándonos las alturas*

viii. *Hasta los ciegos verán allí el jubiloso ascender de su
       Ruego*

ix. *Silenciosos   todos veremos entonces el firmamento
     entero levantarse límpido   iluminado   como una
     playa tendiéndonos el amor constelado de la patria*

THE UTOPIAS

i. The whole desert could be Notre Dame but it was the desert of Chile

ii. All the beaches could be Chartres but they were only the beaches of Chile

iii. All of Chile could be the cathedral Nuestra Señora de Santiago but these arid landscapes were only the evanescent Chilean landscapes

Where the inhabitants of Chile might not be the inhabitants of Chile but a Plea ascending from them until it swept across the sky they watched gently blushing growing transparent as if no one had really looked at their faces

iv. Because the sky might not be the sky but they themselves celestial covering as if it were nothing the arid landscapes they saw

v. Those would have been the gentle inhabitants of Chile silent stooped over populating the chapels of their Plea

vi. They themselves could have been then the peopled chapels of Chile

Where Chile might be not the landscape of Chile but the blue sky that they watched and the landscapes would have been then a Plea without end that escaped from their lips like a long breath released by the whole motherland making a love that would populate their heights

vii. Chile will be then a love populating our heights

viii. Even the blind will see there the joyous ascent of their Plea

ix. Silent we will all see then the whole firmament rise limpid illuminated like a beach offering us the motherland's constellations of love

/*CIII*/

Despertado de pronto en sueños lo oí tras la
noche
"Oye Zurita—me dijo—toma a tu mujer y a tu hijo y te largas de
inmediato"
No macanees—le repuse—déjame dormir en paz, soñaba con unas
montañas que marchan . . .
"Olvida esas estupideces y apúrate—me urgió—no vas a creer que
tienes todo el tiempo del mundo. El Duce se está acercando"
Escúchame—contesté—recuerda que hace mucho ya que me tienes a
la sombra, no intentarás repetirme el cuento. Yo no soy José.
"Sigue las carretera y no discutas. Muy pronto
sabrás la verdad"
Está bien—le repliqué casi llorando—¿y dónde podrá ella alumbrar
tranquila?
Entonces, como si fuera la misma Cruz la que se iluminase, El
contestó:
"Lejos, en esas perdidas cordilleras de Chile"

/CIII/

Awakened suddenly in dreams I heard him beyond the
night
"Hey Zurita," he told me. "Take your wife and your son and
get out of here right now."
"Quit bothering me," I answered. "Let me go back to sleep.
I was dreaming about some mountains that are marching."
"Forget about those stupid things and hurry up," he urged
me.
"Don't think you've got all the time in the world. *Il Duce* is
getting closer."
"Listen to me," I replied. "Remember, you've had me in the
dark for a long time. Don't even try to tell me that story
again. I'm not Joseph."
"Follow the highway and don't argue. You'll know the truth
soon enough."
"All right," I told him almost crying. "And where will she
be able to give birth in peace?"
Then, as if it were the Cross itself that began to shine,
He answered:
"Far away, in those lost cordilleras of Chile."

LAS CORDILLERAS DEL DUCE

Detrás de las costas del Pacífico
negras absolutas
Las cordilleras *del Duce* avanzando

i. *Nada es los Andes para las cordilleras del Duce*

ii. *Más altas pero el viento no amontona nieve sobre ellas*

Abruptas   detrás de las costas del Pacífico   igual que olas que
irrumpieran imponiendo la estatura final de sus montañas ávidas
borrascosas   encrespando los horizontes del oeste

iii. *Porque la muerte era la nieve que encrespaba los*
horizontes del oeste

iv. *Por eso los muertos subían el nivel de las aguas*
amontonados como si se esponjaran sobre ellos

v. *Sólo por eso se levantan desde el otro lado frente a los*
Andes   subidas   empalando el horizonte

Elevándose de su estatura hechas montañas de lágrimas que
encresparan las mejillas de los muertos y todos esos muertos nos
impusieran entonces la subida final de estas aguas

vi. *Por eso sus mejillas son la nieve para las cordilleras del*
Duce

vii. *Igual que nosotros amontonados bajo ellas deshechos*
subiendo la estatura final de las montañas

viii. *Y entonces unos sobre otros todos alcanzamos a ver las*
cordilleras del Duce desprenderse de entre los muertos
enormes absolutas dominando el horizonte

THE CORDILLERAS OF *IL DUCE*

> Behind the pacific coasts
> black absolute
> The cordilleras of *il Duce* advancing

i.   The Andes are nothing for the cordilleras of *il Duce*

ii. Which are higher though the wind piles no snow on top of them

They're rugged behind the Pacific coasts like waves that surge forward imposing the final stature of their mountains avid stormy making whitecaps on the horizons to the west

iii. Because death was the snow that made whitecaps on the horizons to the west

iv. That's why the dead raised the level of the waters piled on top of each other as if they had swelled within them

v.   And that's the only reason why the cordilleras rise from the other side to face the Andes climbing impaling the horizon

Lifting themselves from their stature becoming mountains of tears that made whitecaps on the cheeks of the dead and all those dead imposing on us then the final rising of these waters

vi. That's why their cheeks are the snow for the cordilleras of *il Duce*

vii. The same way that we are piled beneath them undone raising the final stature of the mountains

viii. And then some on top of others we all manage to see the cordilleras of *il Duce* unleash themselves from among the dead enormous absolute dominating the horizon

NIEVES DEL ACONCAGUA

—la muerte—

i. Sudamericanas miren entonces las cumbres andinas

ii. Desde el viento y el frío como ningunas estrellando el cielo contra sus nevados

Tocando los blancos horizontes y las llanuras hasta que sólo un sueño fueron los Andes desplegándose frente a Santiago altos y enfermos en la muerte bañando los enormes cielos sudamericanos

iii. Por eso es tan dulce la muerte sobre la nieve

iv. Porque apenas una nevada es toda esta vida tras los fríos horizontes de las montañas

v. Por eso se levantan sudamericanas ante el cielo y soñando majestuosas de nieve recortándose contra las alturas

Poniéndose más allá del frío y del silencio que se ve mirando la inmensidad blanca de los Andes al otro lado de las nieves en que se bañan los muertos mucho más allá de donde nosotros mismos nos vemos cayendo igual que una helada frente a estas llanuras

vi. Cuando la nieve se levanta y es el sueño la cordillera sudamericana

vii. Donde la vida se va blanqueando en la muerte hasta que sólo un sueño queda de los perdidos horizontes de estos nevados

viii. Cuando pasando como la muerte sobre la nieve todas las cordilleras de los Andes se van a tender sudamericanas y frente al cielo majestuosas heladas perdidas

SNOWS OF ACONCAGUA

death

i. South American peaks look at them then

ii. From the wind and the cold like no others the sky
crashing against their snowcapped peaks

Touching the white horizons and the plains until the Andes
deploying themselves before Santiago were only a dream high and
sick in the death bathing the enormous South American skies

iii. That's why death is so gentle on the snow

iv. Because just one snowfall is this entire life behind the
cold horizons of the mountains

v. That's why the South American peaks rise before the
sky and dream majestic with snow marking a place
for themselves against the heights

Placing themselves beyond the cold and silence one sees while
watching the white immensity of the Andes on the other side of the
snows in which the dead bathe far beyond the place where we
ourselves see each other falling like frost before these plains

vi. When the snow rises and the South American cordilleras
is the dream

vii. Where life erases itself with whiteness in death until
only a dream remains of the lost horizons of these
snowcapped peaks

viii. When passing like death over the snow all the cordilleras
of South America will take their places before the sky
majestic frozen lost

RAÚL ZURITA

VI

Chile está lejano y es mentira
no es cierto que alguna vez nos hayamos prometido
son espejismos los campos
y sólo cenizas quedan de los sitios públicos
Pero aunque casi todo es mentira
sé que algún día Chile entero
se levantará sólo para verte
y aunque nada exista, mis ojos te verán

VI

Chile is far away and is a lie
it isn't true that we ever took our vows
the countryside is a mirage
and only ashes remain of the public places
Because even though almost everything is a lie
I know that someday all of Chile
will rise just to see you
and even if nothing exists, my eyes will see you

DIEGO MAQUIEIRA

(1953)

The religious festival of La Tirana is an unbelievable spectacle that takes place once a year on and around July 16 in a tiny village 80 kilometers from Iquique in northern Chile. The celebration, which is a mixture of pagan and Christian rituals, is based on a legend that has its origin in the sixteenth century. In 1530, Diego de Almagro left Pizarro in Lima and set out to explore the Atacama Desert. According to the story, one of the members of the expedition was an Incan princess/priestess, the Ñusta Huillac. She escaped after her father was killed for planning a revolt and became a despotic ruler of a small community. She was called the Tyrant, *la Tirana*. Later, she captured a Portuguese sailor who was searching for silver, postponed his death sentence, fell in love with him and, just as he converted her to Christianity in order to marry her, was discovered by the rest of the tribe who killed the two lovers in a rain of arrows. As a result of this act of faith, the cult of the Virgen del Carmen de la Tirana was later born. Thousands of dancers with drums and horns descend on the desert town every year to pay tribute to the Virgin.

In the cinematographic series of poems that form Diego Maquieira's book, *La tirana*, the poet adopts many masks. In Chile, this is something that was learned from Nicanor Parra. Maquieira moves in and out of the characters of his namesakes, Almagro and Velázquez, and even becomes a modern version of the Virgin of Tyranny herself. These are poems that combine the most colloquial slang into dense linguistic patterns. While the poems are only nominally linked to the famous religious festival, they do manage to capture the fanaticism, mania and emotional violence associated with it.

Maquieira is from Santiago and does free-lance video work.

NADIE SABE LO QUE YO HABLO

En el pabellón de los santos, yo La Tirana
a fuego cruzado por las entradas
me pego la media volada de mi misma vida
Está la cama, está el retrato de Olivares
sólo dos sábanas transparentadas
al contacto de mi cuerpo:
llena de puntos 50 en cada esquina de salida
de mí misma la fachada del desnudo de Dios
Me caí, estoy empantanada en la belleza
me abro hoyos para que salga mi cuerpo
y me salgan hostias de los hoyos
Me ven soplada por vientos que suben
ya nadie sabe lo que yo hablo
blanca como papel apenas me ven la vida
pues me han sacado de mi más de allá.

NO ONE KNOWS WHAT I'M TALKING ABOUT

In the pavilion of saints, I, the Virgin of Tyranny,
caught by a crossfire from doorways,
took the biggest trip of my life.
There's the bed, there's the portrait of Olivares.
Only two sheets: transparent
when my body touches them.
I'm filled with .50-caliber bullets
from every corner of escape,
from myself, the façade of God's nakedness.
I fell, to sink in the quicksand of my beauty.
I make holes in myself so my body bursts free
and hosts swarm from the holes
(they watch me blow away in rising winds)
no one knows what I'm talking about anymore.
I'm white as paper, they can barely see my life
since they ripped me away from more than beyond.

ME SACARON POR LA CARA

Yo, La Tirana, rica y famosa
la Greta Garbo del cine chileno
pero muy culta y calentona, que comienzo
a decaer, que se me va la cabeza
cada vez que me pongo a hablar
y hacer recuerdos de mis polvos con Veláquez.
Ya no lo hago tan bien como lo hacía antes
Antes, todas las noches y a todo trapo
Ahora no.
Ahora suelo a veces entrar a una Iglesia
cuando no hay nadie
porque me gusta la luz que dan ciertas velas
la luz que le dan a mis pechugas
cuando estoy rezando.
Y es verdad, mi vida es terrible
Mi vida es una inmoralidad
Y si bien vengo de una familia muy conocida
Y si es cierto que me sacaron por la cara
y que los que están afuera me destrozarán
Aún soy la vieja que se los tiró a todos
Aún soy de una ordinariez feroz.

THEY DRAGGED ME OUT BY MY FACE

I'm the Virgin of Tyranny, the rich and famous
Greta Garbo, retired from Chilean films,
the one who's very cultured and hot to trot,
but I'm over the hill
and I'm losing my mind
every time I start to talk
about Velázquez and how I got laid.
I don't do it as well as I used to.
Before, it was every night full speed ahead.
Now, no.
Now, sometimes I go into a Church
when no one's there
because I like the light of certain candles
that light my breasts
when I'm praying.
And it's true, my life is terrible.
My life is immoral.
And even if I do come from a well-known family
and if it's true that they dragged me out by my face
and that the people outside will tear me apart,
I'm still the old lady who fucked them all.
I'm still ordinary—but fierce.

TUS AMIGUITOS ERAN UNOS PERROS

Velázquez de María
tus amiguitos eran unos perros
Habían seis que cuidaban la entrada
de tu casa, y eran de lo peor
Mordían las bergèr sacándoles pedazos
rompían los cuadros de tus nuevos
Givenchy pegados en las tapicerías.
Velázquez, daban vueltas por el living
con una ansiedad que daba miedo
y ya no había cómo pararlos
Ni tú mismo con tus cristos
y tus ruegos de infinita piedad
La raya es que me la daban toda la noche
y me la hicieron bolsa, y además
me sacaron fotos por atrás
para perjudicarme frente a mi familia
Por favor páralos, que no sigan, no es justo
A nadie he dejado triste en esta cama.

YOUR LITTLE FRIENDS WERE A BUNCH OF DOGS

Velázquez de María
your little friends were a bunch of dogs.
There were six of them guarding the doorway
to your house, and they were the worst.
They chewed up your French bergéres,
they ripped apart your new Givenchy
paintings stuck to the tapestries.
Velázquez, they tore through the living room
like they were crazy. I was scared
but there was no way to stop them.
Not even you with your christs
and your pleas of infinite pity.
Worse still, they were at me all night
and left me like a crumpled bag.
Then they took pictures of me from the back
to get me in trouble with my family.
Stop them, please, stop them, it's not fair.
I've never left anyone sad in this bed.

TU GRAN AMOR

Yo te voy a contar la media cochinada
que nos hizo esa noche tu gran amor
Estaba en el Salón Rojo
estaba sentado en su sofá de felpa rojo
viendo Tráiganme la cabeza de Alfredo García
por novena vez sin parar, y rodeado
de su famoso grupito. Y la copia ya la tenía
casi quemada cuando me decidí a entrar
a anunciarle la muerte de Olivares
El mala persona se negó a recibirme
y sus perros me mostraron a la virgen
Me dieron medio segundo para saludar
y de ahí me fui soplada por el hall central
hasta el living, y con riesgo de mi vida
me largué a llorarle la nota oficial
que decía así: Francisco de Olivares
fiestero y cafiche norteamericano
nacido por ahí, vivió en Chile, frecuentó
a Machinegun Kelly, Babyface Nelson
y De María entre otros. Murió loco
esta madrugada en el asilo El Peral
tras haber intentado asesinar a su madre
Y quién te cree Alessandra que a Velázquez
no se le soltó ni el chaleco contra balas.

YOUR GREAT LOVE

I'm gonna tell you how your great love
really fucked us over that night.
He was in the Red Room
sitting on his red felt sofa
watching Bring Me the Head of Alfredo García
for the ninth time without stopping, and surrounded
by his famous bunch. And the copy he had
was almost burned when I decided to come in
to tell him about the death of Olivares.
The bad person refused to receive me
and his dogs showed me the virgin.
They gave me half a second to say hello
and from there I went flying through the central hall
to the living room, and risking my life
I began to cry as I read him the official note
which went like this: Francisco de Olivares,
North American playboy and pimp,
born somewhere, who lived in Chile and hung out
with Machinegun Kelly, Babyface Nelson
and De María, among others, died crazy
today at dawn in the El Peral insane asylum
after trying to murder his mother.
And who would believe you, Alessandra, that Velázquez
in his bulletproof vest didn't even budge.

ME VOLÉ LA VIRGEN DE MIS PIERNAS

Me caía a la cama rosada de su madre
la cama pegada a la pared del baño
Me caí con velos negros en ambos pechos
cada uno entrando a su capilla ardiente
Yo soy la hija de pene, un madre
pintada por Diego Rodríguez de Silva y Velázquez
Mi cuerpo es una sábana sobre otra sábana
el largo de mis uñas del largo de mis dedos
y mi cara de Dios en la cara de Dios
en su hoyo maquillado la cruz de luz:
la que se la suben de ahí, la D.N.A.
la marginada de la taquilla
la que se la están pisando desde 1492
Pero mi cara ya no está más a color
está en mi doble más allá enterrado
con todos mis dedos y mis dientes en la boca
Yo soy Howard Hughes el estilita
me volé la virgen de mis piernas
había pensado tanto en mí misma.

I BLEW UP THE VIRGIN OF MY LEGS

I fell to his mother's pink bed—
the bed stuck to the bathroom wall.
I fell with black candles on both breasts—
each one entering its burning chapel.
I'm the penis's daughter, a mother-man
painted by Diego Rodriguez de Silva y Velázquez.
My body is a sheet on top of another sheet,
the length of my nails as long as my fingers
and my face of God in the face of God,
the cross of light in its cosmetic hole:
I'm the one they lifted over there, the D.N.A.,
the one they kicked out of the thriller,
the one they've been stepping on since 1492.
But my face has no more color.
It's buried in my double beyond
with all my fingers and teeth in my mouth.
I'm Howard Hughes, the hermit.
I blew up the virgin of my legs
having thought so much about myself.

EL GALLINERO

Nos educaron para atrás padre
Bien preparados, sin imaginación
Y malos para la cama.
No nos quedó otra que sentar cabeza
Y ahora todas las cabezas
Ocupan un asiento, de cerdo.

Nos metieron mucho Concilio de Trento
Mucho catecismo litúrgico
Y muchas manos a la obra, la misma
Que en esos años
Repudiaba el orgasmo
Siendo que esta pasta
Era la única experiencia física
Que escapaba a la carne.

Y tanto le debíamos a los Reyes Católicos
Que acabamos con la tradición
Y nos quedamos sin sueños.
Nos quedamos pegados
Pero bien constituidos;
Matrimonios bien constituidos
Familias bien consituidas.

Y así, entonces, nos hicimos grandes:
Aristocracia sin monarquía
Burguesía sin aristocracia
Clase media sin burguesía
Pobres sin clase media
Y pueblo sin revolución.

THE CHICKEN COOP

They taught us backwards, father:
well prepared, with no imaginations
and bad in bed.
We couldn't do anything except bow our heads.
And now all the heads
have a seat—of pigskin.

They filled us with a lot of Council of Trent,
a lot of liturgical catechism
and a lot of God.   The same ones
who in those years
repudiated the orgasm
since this come
was the only physical experience
that escaped from the flesh.

And we owed so much to the Catholic Kings
that we were left without tradition
and without dreams.
We were stuck
but well established—
well-established marriages,
well-established families.

And so, then, we made ourselves great:
aristocracy with no monarchy
bourgeoisie with no aristocracy
middle class with no bourgeoisie
poor with no middle class
and people with no revolution.

CLEMENTE RIEDEMANN
(1953)

The selection of poems that follows was taken from a poetic history called *Karra Maw'n*. The title in *mapudungu*, the language of the Mapuche Indians, means "City of Rain." This series of poems begins with an account of the Indians settling the area that would later be called Valdivia after the arrival of the Spanish conquistadors. In *Karra Maw'n*, the poet adopts the role of the chronicler and recounts the voyages and hardships of his German immigrant ancestors, the destruction of the city by a tidal wave, and the exportation of entire forests on great foreign ships. The epic themes of the poems and their preoccupation with history link them to the work of Ernesto Cardenal.

According to Clemente Riedemann, or Clemens Papa as he is sometimes called, the influence of the Chilean New Song movement on the country's recent poetic production has been underestimated. Riedemann writes lyrics for an excellent folk duo, Schwenke-Nilo. Their provocative songs circulate widely on cassettes and reach an audience that is more diverse than the buyers of poetry books. For Riedemann, the role of the poet (whether it is through songs, the printed or the spoken word) is clear: "Our mission is to tell the world what has happened to us. Our mission is to show the world how we have resolved our problems. Our mission is to offer the world a new language. These are our responsibilities." Riedemann has a degree in anthropological studies of the Mapuche culture. He teaches and lives in Puerto Varas in a house that overlooks Lake Llanquihue and Osorno volcano.

EL ÁRBOL DEL MUNDO

Llegaron ideas desde el norte.
Llegaron de a caballo
            otras técnicas.
    Posaban, unas sobre otras, las piedras
que ya no se movían
            se quedaban fijas
    como estalactitas colgando del cielo boca arriba.

PEDRO DE VALDIVIA: ". . . por hebrero deste
presente año de 1552 poblé la ciudad de Valdivia:
tienen de comer cient vecinos:
no sé coando los hobiere de dar Cédula podrán
                        quedar todos . . ."

    Fue la ciudad con sus torres de piedra,
piedra recogida a la orilla del río.
    No tan corpulentas que pudiere—el español
quebrarse el espinazo.
            No tan flacas que cupieren
más de una entre las manos.

Y luego se lavaban las manos en las aguas del río
        y humedecían con éstas el tallo de los pimientos
y en los huecos de la tierra vertían bochas
        semejantes a los granos de mostaza.

    Ya no sólo las papas.
Más gente con ropas extrañas
        costumbres extrañas
                    cráneos y cacharros de metal.

    Las torres
                árboles catatónicos
en la estructura de un bosque defensivo.
                        Una torre
                EL ÁRBOL DEL MUNDO
"agredir para no ser agredido"

THE TREE OF THE WORLD

From the north came ideas.
On horseback came
            other techniques.
    One on top of the other, the stones
that no longer moved lay still
        fixed
like stalactites hanging from the sky.

*PEDRO DE VALDIVIA: ". . . in February of this
present year of 1552 I populated the city of Valdivia:
    one hundred people have food to eat:
when they must be documented I do not know if all can remain . . ."*

It was the city with its towers of stone,
stone chosen from the banks of the river.
    Not so corpulent so as to break
the Spaniard's spine,
                nor so thin
    that more than one could fit in their hands.

And then they washed their hands in the waters of the river
            and with it moistened the stalks of pimiento trees
and in the hollows of the earth they dropped clusters
        similar to mustard seeds.

Not just potatoes now.
More people with strange clothing
        strange habits
                skulls and pots of metal.

The towers
        catatonic trees
in the structure of a defensive forest.
                    A tower
            THE TREE OF THE WORLD
"attack so as not to be attacked"

Las castellanas plumas en la cumbre de los cascos
no sirvieron para barrer la sangre de los nativos.
Las torres del mundo en la selva sin plumas,

nuevas guerras

mucha sangre antes del trigo
y maremotos
(las aguas subían por la falda de los volcanes
y de los volcanes brotaba el infierno rojo

La primera población marginal de Karra Maw'n.
fue la de los indios
que habían nacido

en Karra Maw'n.

¡WEÑEFE!
¡ÑIÑOKO! —airaban los indios
pero nadie se dio por aludido.
Y LAS TORRES DE SANGRE BAILABAN
EN TORNO AL ÁRBOL DEL MUNDO.

The Castilian plumes from the helmets
were useless for sweeping away the natives' blood.
    The towers of the world in the jungle with no plumes,

                                        new wars

so much blood before the wheat
                        and tidal waves
    (the waters rose over the base of the volcanoes
and from the volcanoes surged the red inferno)

    The first poor section of Karra Maw'n
was where the Indians lived—
                        those who were born
                            in Karra Maw'n.

WEÑEFE!
    ÑIÑOKO!   shouted the Indians in anger
    but no one paid any attention.
AND THE TOWERS OF BLOOD DANCED
            AROUND THE TREE OF THE WORLD.

EL HOMBRE DE LEIPZIG

El padre del padre de mi padre traía todo el mar en sus mejillas. Trajo un cormorán en la mirada y una flauta dulce en los bolsillos.

No trajo papeles, ni osamentas. Le quitaron su historia en las aduanas y venía de lejos.

Al llegar, sólo la niebla, pañal de maíz para envolver los viejos barcos de madera: la "Steinward," el "Hermann," el bergantín "Susanne" y el "Alfred." Todos buscando el paraíso. Para todos, desengaño y selva.

(El daguerrotipo muestra a unas familias apiñadas y sin saber a qué atenerse. Allí dormitan en el suelo el hacedor de calamorros y la mujer del peluquero. También, un niño con paperas).

¡Oh viejos barcos de madera! ¡Oh germánicos famélicos! Les prometieron la tierra, pero la tierra tenía dueños falsos. Falsas estacas de papel y no auténticos rewes milenarios. El padre del padre de mi padre hubo de hablar en otra lengua, gotear de nuevo el semen de la aurora. A fundar cosas es que vino el hombre de tan lejos.

Corral, después de un siglo, pronuncio tu nombre en la mañana. Estoy de pie sobre una lancha arrojando trozos de carne podrida a las gaviotas. Por aquí entró en América el perseguido, uno que no fue rico ni famoso, sino bello. Porque bello es todo cuanto sigue siendo, a pesar de la muerte, el deterioro y el olvido.

El hombre de Leipzig, el carpintero, me trajo a tierra en el lápiz de su oreja, de donde he bajado para organizar el mundo con palabras.

THE MAN FROM LEIPZIG

The father of my father's father brought all the sea in his cheeks. He carried a cormorant in his eyes and a smooth flute in his pockets.

He brought no papers or skeletons. At customs they took away his past—and he came from far away.

When he arrived, he was greeted only by fog, cloth of corn, wrapping the old wooden boats: the "Steinward," the "Hermann," the brigantine "Susanne," and the "Alfred." Everyone was looking for paradise. But they only found deception and jungle.

(The daguerrotype shows a cluster of families who didn't know where they could turn. The cobbler and the barber's wife sleep on the dirt floor. So does a child with mumps.)

Oh, old wooden boats! Oh, starving Germans! They promised you land, but the land had false gods. It was staked on paper but had no authentic *rewes** that would last for thousands of years. The father of my father's father had to speak another language, drip with the semen of the dawn again. To carve his own niche, he came from so far away.

Corral, a century later I say your name in the morning. I'm standing in a boat throwing pieces of rotten meat to the gulls. Here, someone who was persecuted entered America, someone who wasn't rich or famous—only beautiful. Because what goes on living in spite of death, decay and oblivion is beautiful.

The man from Leipzig, the carpenter, brought me to this land on the pencil behind his ear and I have come down to organize the world with words.

---

*the sacred stairways of wood used by *la machi*, the priestess/shaman of the Mapuche Indians

EL SUEÑO DEL WEKUFE

Wekufe está durmiendo.
Y el Gran Señor Chaw-Ngënechén
           SER DIVINO
  hace de las suyas.
  Ahora están brotando flores:
           Pewén
  Kolkopi-Chol cho
    Klon Maki
    (arbusto)

pequeñas flores que alimentan
más que la venganza y la vergüenza.

Los habitantes de Karra Maw'n
cruzan el puente hacia la isla.
Y desde el puente se aprecian
competencias de botes
    truchas
        cebollas
  mariposas que en los botes se venden
al mejor postor
  y al mejor pintor
quienes recrean la historia de los sucesivos despojos.

Allí donde el malecón
sobre tibios esqueletos se yergue
  un niño mapuche se arrodilla y habla:
    "mi casa no se cayó
    porque la hice con tierra y paja.
    No se cayó mi casa
    porque la hice yo."

  Para ángeles y asesinos
son las medallas
  que el acuñador extrae de sus moldes

        ¡MAW'N, MAW'N!
        —dicen las gaviotas.

Bendice, lluvia
  estas palabras:
¡MAW'N MAW'N!

WEKUFE'S DREAM

Wekufe is sleeping.
And the great Lord Chaw-Ngënechen
                              DIVINE BEING
   does what he likes.
   Now flowers are sprouting:
                              Pewén
      Kolkopi-Chol cho
         Klon Maki
         (bush)

small flowers that feed more
   than vengeance and shame.

The inhabitants of Karra Maw'n
cross the bridge toward the island.
   And from the bridge they can see
boat races
                Trout
                       Onions
   butterflies sold in the boats
to the highest bidder
   and to the best painter
to those who recreate the history of the successive looting.

There, where the waterfront steps
rise over warm skeletons,
   a mapuche boy kneels and speaks:
                "My house didn't fall
         because I made it with earth and straw.
                My house didn't fall
            because I made it myself."

   The medals extracted
from the minter's molds
   are only for angels and assassins
                       MAW'N, MAW'N!
                       —cry the gulls.

   Bless these words,
         rain:
   MAW'N, MAW'N!

Bendice tu propia boca
y luego déjate caer con propósitos benignos.
Para que te levantes y vuelvas
convertido en espiga de acero
en manantial que humedezca el canelo de los deseos.

¡*MAW'N, MAW'N!*
Pero no hay mapuches.
Lo que hay
es medio millón de arrinconados.
La Ley dice: "No hay mapuches. Somos todos chilenos."

Y somos chilenos
y estamos tristes
habitando la esfera única
que no se cansa de girar sobre su eje
llevando a cuestas
los colores de mil jardines diferentes
pequeñas flores que enrojecen
junto a los grandes árboles del bosque.

La diversidad hizo posible la belleza.
Que el Sol nunca llegue a estar en manos de ningún gobierno.

Y en la torre,
si apegas el oído al muro de la torre
oirás el rugido de los tokis
y caballos traspasados por el hierro

"¡*MAW'N, MAW'N!*"
—*dentro de la torre,*
el sueño del Wekufe
con su cintillo de plata
DURMIENDO DENTRO DE LA TORRE.

Bless your own mouth and then
let yourself fall with benign designs.
   So that you rise and change
into spikes of steel
   into a fountain that waters the *canelo* tree of desires.

MAW'N, MAW'N!
But there are no mapuches.
   What there is
      is half a million neglected people.
The Law says: *"There are no mapuches: we're all Chileans."*

And we are Chileans
and we're sad inhabitants of a single sphere
   that never tires of spinning on its axis
carrying on its back
   the colors of thousands of different gardens
small flowers getting redder
   next to the forest's enormous trees.

Diversity made beauty possible.
   Let the sun never fall into the hands of any government.

   And in the tower,
if you press your ear to the wall of the tower
   you will hear the tokis roar
      and horses run through by iron

                        "MAW'N, MAW'N!"
                        —inside the Tower,
Wekufe dreaming
   with his silver headband
      SLEEPING INSIDE THE TOWER.

Notes: *Wekufe* is a diabolical spirit of the Mapuches. *Pewén* is the indigenous name for the araucaria pine, *kolkopi-Chol cho* is the copihue—the national flower of Chile. *Tokis* are Indian military chiefs during times of war.

TERESA CALDERÓN

(1955)

Teresa Calderón's studied approach to writing produces an exactness and imperturbability in her work. The tension between the future and the past in poems such as "Of the Nameless Birds" and "Face to Face in another Time" lies in the mystery of unanswered questions and the problems in human relationships that will never be resolved. The poetry of Teresa Calderón appeared in the anthology *Uno x uno* and, in 1982, she received a prize in the Gabriela Mistral poetry competition. She finished her studies in pedagogy at the Universidad Católica and currently works as a teacher in Santiago.

DE LAS AVES SIN NOMBRE

Y mañana,
qué será mañana de los rostros
que inventé para buscarme,
de las palabras que no pude
imaginar en mi presencia.

Mañana, pregunto,
que será de la tierra
llovida de araucarias
y del ave sin nombre
que mordía los ciruelos
más allá del cemento y los alambres.

Mañana,
qué será el refugio pensativo
entre los tilos,
aquellos que esperaban tanto
algún regreso,
qué será
del beso que dejaron
envuelto en las violetas
y parpadea todavía
como un secreto entre nosotros.

Y mañana
qué será de la lluvia
que entibiaba los manzanos
a la vuelta de los ojos.

¿Será la vida, tal vez,
un crepúsculo infinito,
y la calle
un inmenso espejo inmóvil?

OF THE NAMELESS BIRDS

And tomorrow,
tomorrow what will become of the faces
I invented to look for me,
of the words I couldn't
imagine in my presence.

Tomorrow, I ask,
what will become of the earth
where the araucaria pines rain down
and of the nameless bird
that pecked at plums
beyond cement and barbed wire.

Tomorrow,
what will become of the refuge
where I think among the lindens,
the ones that waited so long
for someone to return.
What will become of the kiss
they left tangled in violets
and still blinks there
like a secret we share.

And tomorrow,
what will become of the rain
that warmed the apple trees
when the eyes come back.

Will life be
an endless dusk, perhaps,
and the street
a great, immobile mirror?

DEDUCCIONES

1
Los ciegos tienen ojos hacia adentro.
Tienen suerte.

2
El hombre se encomienda a Dios.
Cede el olmo en su alto rama.
Se condena.

3
No todo lo que reluce es hombre.
El ídolo de barro se baña en la laguna.

4
La luz inunda la sala.
Alguien pregunta.
Pero la noche acude puntual.

5
Un día es mucho tiempo.
El silencio tiene la palabra -todavía-.
La pregunta flota en el aire
de la última pregunta.

6
Nadie tiene razón.
El laberinto, sin duda,
no conduce al Minotauro.

7
Pertenecen al pasado
los hombres temblando ante el suceso
del Pájaro o la Flor.

8
Tu recuerdo obstaculiza mis mejores
intenciones.
La voluntad es un reino que me queda lejos.

DEDUCTIONS

1
The blind have eyes within.
They're lucky.

2
Man entrusts himself to God.
The elm yields in its highest branches.
He condemns himself.

3
Not everything that glitters is a man.
The clay idol bathes in the pond.

4
Light floods the room.
Someone asks a question.
But the night arrives on time.

5
One day is a long time.
Silence has the floor—still.
The question floats in the air
of the last question.

6
No one is right.
The labyrinth, without a doubt,
does not lead to the Minotaur.

7
Whoever trembles before the phenomenon
of the Bird or the Flower
belongs to the past.

8
Your memory blocks my best intentions.
Volition is a kingdom I may not reach.

9
Y suena el olvido como un cuerno
en las noches más antiguas
guerra adentro.

10
Extinguida la función
los actores se abandonan a sí mismos.
Nadie tiene claro
si en verdad el supuesto se termina
o recomienza más allá de los tinglados
en las horas de oficina.

11
Arrestado en su domicilio
a medianoche
mientras pensaba
sorprendido "de facto"
en clandestina asamblea
consigo mismo.

9
Oblivion sounds its horn
on the most ancient nights
entering the war.

10
Once the show is extinguished,
the actors abandon themselves.
No one knows for sure
if what had been supposed really ends
or begins again beyond the makeshift stage
during the hours at the office.

11
Arrested in his home
as he thought
at midnight
surprised "de facto"
in a clandestine gathering
with himself.

NUNCA SUPE

1

A espaldas de cualquier pregunta,
con las hojas más pequeñas de la luz
se ejecuta la sombra en los objetos.

Ya no hay nada que hacer.
Me inquieta esa puerta y la traspaso.
Nunca supe
que queriendo salir
estaba entrando inevitablemente.

2

Hay tantos caminos que conducen
hacia adentro.
Cuesta distinguir
el exacto aleteo de la luz.
¿Es la sombra la elegida
o es la claridad
el destino ineludible de la sombra?

Nada es absoluto.
No hay que estar, sin embargo,
muy seguros de las cosas.
Pareciera suficiente saber nombrarlas
o balbucear de algún modo su presencia.

I NEVER REALIZED

1
Back turned to any question,
with leaves smaller than light,
the shadow in objects is made.

Nothing more can be done.
That door disturbs me and I go through it.
I never realized
that, wanting to leave,
I was inevitably entering.

2
There are so many roads
that lead within.
It's hard to discern
the exact wingbeat of light.
Is shadow the one to choose
or is clarity
the unavoidable destiny of shadow?

Nothing is absolute.
There's no need, nevertheless,
to be very sure about things.
It seems enough to know how to name them
or somehow babble them into existence.

EL TIEMPO QUE TODO LO DESTRUYE

Se está batiendo en retirada.
Sin aviso por el cielo
se avecina la pregunta
asediada
por viejos espejismos
y detrás de los ojos
se escabulle.

En tanto, van cayendo
los minutos
uno a uno traicionados,
hacia adentro,
por la puerta
lateral del invierno,
despavoridamente humanos,
adormeciéndose,
en el lado oscuro de la muerte.

THE TIME THAT DESTROYS EVERYTHING

Wings its way into the distance.
Without warning in the sky
the question comes closer
besieged
by old mirages
and slips in
behind our eyes.

Meanwhile, the minutes
fall, betrayed,
one by one
within us
through the side
door of winter,
frighteningly human,
falling asleep
on the dark side of death.

CÓDIGO DE AGUAS

La lluvia
se dedicó a llover
desconsolada.
Trajo un canto perdido
acunado en subterráneos.
Vino hiriendo
las tejas de los años,
las rodillas de un niño,
con ojos fijos
llegó a beber en la conciencia.
Después formará túneles,
crecerá por encima del ladrillo
y el agua
se esconderá en la tierra
como los muertos.

CODE OF WATERS

The rain,
disconsolate,
devoted itself
to raining.
It brought a lost song
cradled underground.
It came, wounding
the red rooftops of the years,
the knees of a child.
With unblinking eyes
it drank from our conscience.
Later it will form tunnels,
flow across brick
and the water
will hide in the earth
like the dead.

PURO SUCEDER DE MIRADAS ANTERIORES

Perdíamos el tiempo diseñando navíos
que jamás llegarían al mar,
construyendo territorios ilegibles
hasta cuando la casa se cayó en el viento,
y las palabras escaparon hacia nunca
por el cielo derrumbado.

Eramos, sin duda, la lejanía,
menuda calma sin acceso a la Historia,
creyéndonos visiones
en los ojos de otros ojos,
dos fantasmas deshabitando el bosque,
porque nunca Amor fue suficiente
y su luz se la llevaron a picotazos.

Parecía difícil laberinto,
tú mirando las cosas solamente para ti,
y yo disfrazada de pájaros huyendo
en tu busca,
mirándonos siempre de frente
sin poder encontrarnos.

FACE TO FACE IN ANOTHER TIME

We wasted time designing boats
that would never reach the sea,
building illegible territories
until the time when the house fell in the wind
and the words escaped toward never
through the crumbling sky.

We were, without a doubt, the distance,
the minute calm without access to History,
believing ourselves visions
in the eyes of other eyes,
two phantoms vacating the forest,
Because Love was never enough
and its light was carried away
in the beaks of birds.

It seemed like a difficult maze—
you looked at things just for yourself
and I, disguised as fleeing birds,
searched for you.
Face to face
never able to find each other.

ARISTÓTELES ESPAÑA

(1955)

Equilibrios e incomunicaciones by Aristóteles España belongs to the genre of testimonial literature best exemplified by writers such as Nazim Himket, Marcos Ana and Roque Dalton. The following poems were written in the concentration camp on Dawson Island, Chile between September of 1973 and July of 1974. As a 17-year old regional student leader and supporter of the Popular Unity government headed by Salvador Allende, España was arrested during the military coup in Punta Arenas, Chile's southernmost important city located on the Straits of Magellan, and sent by boat to the isolated prison on Dawson Island. España was the youngest of prisoners including many important ministers of the Allende government such as Orlando Letelier and José Tohá.

The notebooks of poems that described daily life in the concentration camp, the torture sessions, the beatings, the humiliation, the fear and pain, the hope and comradeship were smuggled from the prison and published clandestinely in Punta Arenas in 1975. Subsequent anonymous, mimeographed editions followed in 1980 and 1982. The first copy I received of the book was a series of typewritten, photocopied pages bound between two heavy steel bars. España won the 1983 Gabriela Mistral Poetry Prize.

LLEGADA

Bajamos de la barcaza con las manos en alto
a una playa triste y desconocida.
La primavera cerraba sus puertas,
el viento nocturno sacudió de pronto
mi cabeza rapada
el silencio,
esa larga fila de Confinados
que subía a los camiones de la Armada Nacional
marchando
cerca de las doce de la noche del once de septiembre
de mil novecientos setenta y tres en Isla Dawson.
Viajamos
por un camino pantanoso que me pareció
una larga carretera con destino a la muerte.
Un camino con piedras y soldados.
El ruido del motor es una carcajada,
mi abrigo café tiene barro y bencina:
nos rodean
bajamos del camión
uno   dos   tres   kilómetros
cerca
del
mar
y
de
la
nada,
¿Qué será de Chile a esta hora?
¿Veremos el sol mañana?
Se escuchan voces de mando y entramos a un callejón
esquizofrénico que nos lleva al Campo de Concentración,
se encienden focos amarillos a nuestro paso,
las ventanas de la vida se abren y se cierran.

ARRIVAL

We step from the barge, hands in the air,
onto a sad and unknown beach.
Spring closed its doors,
the night-wind suddenly shook
        my shaved head,
        silence,
that long line of Prisoners
climbing into the trucks of the National Armada
        marching
at about midnight on September eleventh,
nineteen hundred and seventy-three on Dawson Island.
We traveled a marshy road that made me
think of a long highway toward death.
A road with stones and soldiers.
The motor bursts out laughing.
My brown jacket covered with mud reeks of gasoline.
        They surround us.
        We get off the truck
one   two   three   kilometers
        by
        sea
        and
        no-
        thing.
I wonder what's happening in Chile now.
Will we see the sun tomorrow?
Voices shout orders and we enter
a schizophrenic alley that takes us to the Concentration Camp.
Yellow spotlights flare as we pass.
The windows of life open and close.

INFIERNO Y SOLEDAD

Han pasado ya trescientas horas
—más o menos—
y algunos leves nubarrones,
estornudos, azotes,
los Agentes de Seguridad no nos dejan dormir,
interrogan y torturan
a la luz de la luna y de las linternas.
El Comandante comunicó
que somos prisioneros de guerra,
que el Presidente ha muerto,
que seremos tratados de acuerdo
a los Convenios de Ginebra.
La noche se da vueltas en su cama:
Son escenas difíciles de describir en estas líneas.
Pienso en un árbol de Pascua gigantesco
aquí en la Isla, y con juguetes.
El mundo es una empresa privada,
nuestro comedor es una carpa de campaña.
Colocan diarios murales en el patio.
Leemos: "Fusilados cinco extremistas"
          "Se construye una Patria Nueva."
Trotamos todas las mañanas,
hacemos flexiones,
"sapitos,"
después nos lavamos en el río,
nos enseñan cantos militares;
un sargento me dice: "No te metas más en tonterías."
Tenemos deseos de jugar fútbol,
queremos cansarnos y dormir,
soñar, jugar al naipe,
ya llegará el momento del análisis,
es preciso salir vivos,
la verdad nos espera con sus piernas abiertas.

HELL AND SOLITUDE

Three hundred hours have gone by
-more or less-
and some weightless thunderheads,
the sneezing, the sting of the whip,
the Security Agents will not let us sleep.
They interrogate and torture
by moonlight and lanterns.
The Commandant tells us
we're prisoners of war,
the President is dead,
and that we'll be treated according
to the rules of the Geneva Convention.
The night tosses and turns in its bed.
Difficult scenes to describe in these lines.
I'm thinking about a giant Christmas tree
here on the Island—and toys.
The world is a private enterprise.
Our dining room is an army tent.
They post newspapers and murals.
We read them: "Five Extremists Shot"
                    "A New Country Is Built"
We jog every morning
and do exercises
("squat thrusts").
Then we bathe in the river.
They teach us military songs:
a sergeant tells me, "Keep out of trouble."
We feel like playing soccer,
we want to get tired and sleep,
dream, play cards.
Soon enough the moment of analysis will come.
We've got to get out alive.
The truth is waiting for us with her parted legs.

CAMINOS

Nos llevan a cortar leña por los bosques,
de sol a sol,
custodiados por patrullas
que apuntan directamente a la cabeza,
ordenan cantar y correr,
agujerean nuestra sensibilidad,
quieren destruirnos como guijarros
bajo la nieve,
humillarnos,
mientras entonamos en alta voz:
"Bajo la linterna, frente a mi cuartel,
Sé que tu me esperas mi dulce amada bien . . ."
Y el viento invade los parques de mis sombras,
desordena los faroles, las plantas escarchadas.
Me acuerdo de Rosita en la última navidad,
o con su uniforme de colegiala y sus cuadernos.
(A lo mejor nunca leerá este poema)
Hay olor a nubes enterradas,
nos golpean,
mientras una rata camina entre la hierba . . .
"Si e que llega un parte y debo yo marchar
Sin saber querida si podré regresar . . ."
Solo vemos galerías pintadas de insomnio,
postes amontonados,
manos que sangran,
hoyos,
vómitos,
en el trayecto al Campo de Detenidos,
y fusiles,
y mitades,
encerrados en un laberinto de crueldad y miseria
en el paralelo 53 de este mundo.

ROADS

They take us to chop wood in the forests
from sun to sun.
Watched by patrols
pointing weapons at our heads.
Ordered to sing and run.
They riddle our sense of self-worth.
They want to destroy us like pebbles
beneath the snow,
humiliate us
while we sing in loud voices:
In the light of the lantern by my barracks door,
I know you'll be waiting for me, my love . . .
And the wind invades the parks of my shadows,
whipping the streetlights and the plants covered with frost.
I remember Rosita last Christmas
dressed in her high school uniform with her notebooks.
(Perhaps she'll never read this poem)
The smell of buried clouds:
they beat us
while a rat scurries through the grass . . .
If the orders come, and I must go,
when I'll be back, my love, you'll never know . . .
We see only the painted galleries of insomnia,
pole after pole,
bleeding hands,
holes,
vomit,
in the journey through the Prison Camp,
and guns,
and halves,
locked in a labyrinth of cruelty and misery
on the 53rd parallel of this world.

APUNTES

Me fotografían en un galpón
como a un objeto,
uno, dos, tres veces,
de perfil, de frente,
confeccionan mi ficha con esmero:
"soltero, estudiante, 17 años,
peligroso para la Seguridad
del Estado."
Miran de reojo:
Quieren mis huellas las dactilares.
Un sudor helado
inunda mis mejillas.
No he comido.
Creo que hay una tormenta.
Me engrillan nuevamente.
Tengo náuseas.
Empiezo a ver que todo gira
a mil kilómetros por hora.
Se estrellan sus puños
en mis oídos.
Caigo.
Grito de dolor.
Voy a chocar con una montaña.
Pero no es una montaña.
Sino barro y puntapiés,
y un ruido intermitente
que se mete en mi cerebro
Hasta la inconciencia.

NOTES

They photograph me in a large shed
as if I were an object,
one, two, three times.
The profile, the front,
they prepare my dossier with great care:
"single, student, 17 years old,
dangerous to the Security
of the State."
They look at me
out of the corners of their eyes:
they want my fingerprints.
A cold sweat
washes across my cheeks.
I haven't eaten.
I think there's a storm.
They slap me in chains again.
I feel sick to my stomach.
Everything starts to spin past
at a thousand kilometers per hour.
Their fists shatter
against my ears.
I fall.
I cry out in pain.
I'm going to crash into a mountain.
But it's not a mountain—
just mud and the boots that kick me,
and an intermittent sound
that slips into my brain
as I lose consciousness.

ENGRANAJES

Este miércoles se le agotaron las pilas al firmamento,
octubre moja su cola entre las olas,
Pablo Neruda ha muerto,
el tiempo se deshace en las literas,
seguramente continúan los fusilamientos,
pasado mañana cumplo dieciocho años,
América es un torbellino,
volverán los yanquis,
nos mantienen en una constante incertidumbre
frecuentemente nos visita un sacerdote,
anoche soñé que bailaba un tango en la penumbra,
¿Cómo será el rostro de los torturadores?
las ampolletas de la barraca están encendidas,
estamos acostados,
se apagan las luces,
la alegría y la libertad
deben ser como dos muchachas bonitas.

WIRE MESHES

This Wednesday the sky ran out of batteries,
October dips its tail in the waves,
Pablo Neruda is dead,
time dissolves on the cots,
most likely more people will be shot,
the day after tomorrow I'll be eighteen,
America is a whirlwind,
the *yanquis* will return,
they keep us in constant uncertainty,
a priest visits us often,
last night I dreamed I was dancing a tango in the shadows.
What does the face of the torturers look like?
The lightbulbs in the barracks are lit,
we're lying down,
the lights go off,
happiness and freedom
must be like two pretty girls.

MÁS ALLÁ DE LA TORTURA

Fuera del espacio y la materia,
en una región altiva (sin matices ni colores)
llena de un humo horizontal
que atraviesa pantanos invisibles,
permanezco sentado
como un condenado a la cámara de gas.
Descubro
que el temor es un niño desesperado,
que la vida es una gran habitación
o un muelle vacío en medio del océano.
Hay disparos,
ruidos de máquinas de escribir,
me aplican corriente eléctrica en el cuerpo.
Soy
un extraño pasajero en viaje a lo desconocido,
arden mis uñas y los poros, los tranvías,
en la sala contigua golpean a una mujer embarazada,
las flores del amor y la justicia
cercerán más adelante sobre las cenizas
de todas las dictaduras de la tierra.

BEYOND TORTURE

Outside of space and matter
in a proud place (without tone or color)
filled with horizontal smoke
that crosses invisible swamps
I remain seated
like a person condemned to the gas chamber.
I discover
that fear is a desperate child,
that life is a great room
or a deserted dock in the middle of the ocean.
Gunfire,
sounds of typewriters,
they apply the electric current to my body.
I am
a strange traveler journeying toward the unknown.
My nails and pores burn, the streetcars
in the next room strike a pregnant woman.
The flowers of love and justice
will grow sometime later from the ashes
of all the dictatorships on earth.

INTIMO

Amor, la sangre forma un riachuelo
aquí en la soledad del "Container,"
el dolor es un enorme látigo
que azota mis dudas y relámpagos.
Pasan segundos,
pequeñas eras de vértigo,
Edades que me recuerdan tus labios
en nuestras dulces tardes de junio.
Hoy, todo tiene un sentido telúrico,
subterráneo, inmensamente agrio,
los cuerpos de mis compañeros en el piso,
el ruido de los tanques en la tarde,
las arañas anidan cerca de nosotros,
este sucio papel donde escribo.

INTIMATE

My love, the blood trickles away
here in the solitude of "The Container,"
pain is an enormous whip
striking my doubts and bolts of lightning.
Seconds pass,
tiny eras of vertigo,
ages that remind me of your lips
on our sweet June afternoons.
Today, everything has an earthen,
subterranean, immensely bitter taste.
The bodies of my *compañeros* on the floor.
The sound of the tanks in the afternoon.
The spiders that spin their webs near us.
This dirty paper where I write.

LA VENDA

La venda es un trozo de oscuridad
que oprime,
un rayo negro que golpea las tinieblas,
los íntimos gemidos de la mente,
penetra como una aguja enloquecida,
la venda,
en las duras estaciones de la ira
y el miedo,
hiriendo, desconcertando,
se agrandan las imágenes,
los ruidos son campanas
que repican estruendosamente,
la venda,
es un muro cubierto de espejos y musgos,
un cuarto deshabitado,
una escalera llena de incógnitas,
la venda
crea una atmósfera fantasmal,
ayuda a ingresar raudamente
a los pasillos huracanados
de la meditación y el pánico.

THE BLINDFOLD

The blindfold is a slice of darkness
that oppresses,
a black beam of light striking shadows,
the intimate moaning of the mind.
It penetrates like an insane needle:
the blindfold.
In the hard seasons of anger
and fear
it wounds and bewilders.
Images get bigger.
Sounds are bells
tolling and tolling.
The blindfold
is a wall covered with mirrors and moss,
a room where no one lives,
a stairway to the unknown.
The blindfold
fills the air with phantoms
and helps blast open the way
to the hurricaned corridors
of meditation and panic.

QUÉ HACER EN ESTA HORA

Qué hacer en esta hora,
caminar dentro de la celda,
dar vueltas,
regresar al vientre de la idea,
irse definitivamente
al rincón más oscuro de la angustia
o ver más allá de este minuto,
buscar una respuesta,
abrir las ventanas
de este momento,
reflexionar mirando
las vertientes de la historia.

WHAT SHOULD I DO NOW?

What should I do now?
Walk in the cell,
pace,
return to the womb of the idea,
head straight
for the darkest corner of anguish
or look beyond this minute,
search for an answer,
open the windows
of this moment,
reflect, consider
the watersheds of history.

(NO HAY MÁS DOLOR BAJO LOS ÁRBOLES)

Estamos arriba de un camión
-y ese camión es como toda la tierra-
se mueve alrededor de un sol
más triste que el rostro de un niño muerto.

Avanza el camión
como un fantasma por la isla.

Un soldado nos golpea en las sienes,
en los testículos,

nos amarran.

El camión se detiene en la playa.
Nos desnudan.
Caminamos vendados por la arena,
la arena es un clavo que hiere
y rasga nuestros dedos,
hacen preguntas,
escupen nuestros rostros,
nos botan en lo más hondo de la mierda,
vomitamos en el pozo,
ellos ríen como locos
y se van en el camión hacia su infierno.

Los ojos de la vida con sus lágrimas
limpian lentamente nuestros cuerpos.

(NO GREATER PAIN BENEATH THE TREES)

We're inside a truck
—and that truck is like the entire Earth—
circling a sun
sadder than the face of a dead child.

The truck moves
like a phantom across the island.

A soldier strikes our foreheads,
our testicles.

They tie us up.

The truck stops on the beach.
They strip us.
We walk blindfolded on the sand.
The sand is a nail that cuts
and rips our toes.
They ask us questions.
They spit on our faces.
They dump us into the deepest part of the shit.
We vomit in the hole.
They laugh like crazy
and leave in the truck toward their hell.

The eyes of life with their tears
slowly clean our bodies.

UNA ESPECIE DE CANTO

He aprendido a amar entre barrotes
rodeado de secretos, amenazas,
a conocer los metales del desprecio,
el valor de la unidad y la palabra,
a sentir,
a ser valiente cuando me torturan,
contemplar como crecen las semillas
en las jaulas . . .
He aprendido a distinguir los cánticos
del odio,
nacer, caminar entre la bruma
y crecer,
y escuchar risas que evocan garras,
muecas, los pasos del verdugo,
el temblor bullicioso de mis venas . . .
He aprendido a ver las simas
transparentes de lo humano,
el helado resplandor de la ternura,
la otra dimensión de la esperanza.

A KIND OF SONG

I've learned to love between bars
surrounded by secrets, threats,
to recognize the metals of contempt,
the value of unity and words,
to feel,
to be brave when they torture me,
to contemplate the way seeds grow
in the cages . . .
I've learned to distinguish the canticles
of hatred,
to be born, to walk in the fog
and to grow
and to listen to laughter that evokes claws,
faces twisted in pain, the executioner's footsteps,
the roaring of my veins . . .
I've learned to see
the transparent abysses of what's human,
the cold splendor of compassion,
the other dimension of hope.

PARTIDA

Me avisan que debo alistar mi maleta,
ordenar las frazadas,
quedo mudo y perplejo.
No me atrevo a despedirme.
Somos un grupo numeroso.
¿A dónde vamos?
Se cruzan nuestras miradas,
escondo mi cuaderno,
son momentos de mucha intensidad,
me duele el estómago,
hay un gran despliegue de tropas,
inusual y desmedido,
surgen conjeturas,
caen granizos,
todo se llena de ausencias,
escribo mis iniciales en la pared.
Afuera hay un vehículo con destino desconocido
y después una lancha torpedera o un avión,
hay cierta claridad glacial
que va blanqueando nuestro andar;
veo orillas que se hunden como barcos,
troncos quemados,
hombres que entran y salen de sí mismos.
Siento un leve escozor en las rodillas,
cierro mis párpados ahora.
Hasta siempre, camaradas,
toda esta lección no ha sido en vano.

LEAVING

They tell me I should pack my suitcase,
fold my blankets.
I'm silent and perplexed.
I don't dare say goodbye.
There are many of us.
Where are we going?
A crisscrossing of glances.
I hide my notebook.
Intense moments.
My stomach hurts.
A great deployment of troops,
unusual, out of proportion.
Rumors fly.
Hail falls.
Everything fills with absences.
I write my initials on the wall.
Outside, a vehicle with an unknown destination
and afterwards a torpedo boat or a plane.
There's a certain glacial clarity
erasing our steps with whiteness.
I see shorelines sinking like boats,
burnt tree trunks,
men who go in and out of themselves.
I feel a slight pain in my knees.
I close my eyes now.
We'll see each other again, always, comrades.
All we've learned has not been in vain.

GONZALO MUÑOZ

(1956)

As the poet warns in a reference to Maurice Blanchot at the beginning of his first book, *Exit*, "language is not presence, but absence." Gonzalo Muñoz's poetry is highly experimental and difficult to penetrate. In *Exit*, the influence of the cinema plays an important part in the fragmented structure of the book and the way the text leaps from scene to scene. The ambiguity of the text with its androgynous characters moving from one ritualistic sequence to another hides what is tangible or keeps it just beyond the reader's grasp. The fragments in Muñoz's second book, *Este*, from which the selection presented here is taken, have been consolidated into a columnar form. The poems chosen are a miniature version of the entire book in its movement from single to double columns after passing through the white, red and blue colors of the Chilean flag. Gonzalo Muñoz resides in Santiago, teaches and free lances as a graphic designer.

ESTE (Selecciones)

/. . . bajo las rocas pastan los olvidados
animales muertos, se siguen silenciosos,
apretados contra el muro, emiten voces
(sobre ellos ha caído alguna culpa pues
los buscan a todos) y alucinados se esca-
bullen con sus lanas manchadas de rojo se-
co. son marcas en la distancia, deambulan-
do entre las piedras atravesadas del vien-
to seco del este.
esos príncipes venidos de las alturas a
perder la piel en las alambradas, cerca-
dos por reflectores, ahora miran hacia
los montes que adoraron y descubren:
blanco, el lugar perdido.
antes los dirigieron a los caminos y aho-
ra ya sin dirección ese tránsito, ese
vagabundeo, ese extravío es lo que amena-
za los sueños. según informes: creyeron
que se habían ido a lo largo de los valles
escapando, fugados o asolados por la duda,
caídos a las aguas correntosas, estrella-
dos en los desfiladeros. otros repitieron
estas narraciones, hicieron circular escri-
tos falsos.
sorpresiva ahora esa presencia muerta,
creciendo, multiplicándose en su última
reunión callada, desplazándose en silencio,
pisoteando la yerba pobre.
sólo sus respiros entrecortados, AH, AH, AH
sus exhalaciones enfermas
(esa piel de otra piel que roza toda manta rota)

LOS FOTOGRAFIARON DESDE EL AIRE PARA UBICAR
SUS SANTUARIOS   - SABER DONDE TIRAR -

identifica su propia figura desnuda sufrien-
te, en el cubo blanco donde yace vertical,
atravesado de luces y sombras, silencioso,
en el olvido de ese lecho
*   - creyó ser santo -*

EAST (Selections)

/ . . . beneath the rocks the forgotten dead animal
graze, following each other in silence, pressed
against the wall, uttering words (some kind of
guilt has fallen over them since they all are
being sought), slipping into hallucination with
their wool stained a dry red.   they are branded
spots in the distance, wandering among the stones
split by the dry wind from the east.
those princes who came from the heights to lose
their skin on barbed wire, surrounded by search-
lights, look now toward the hills they adored
and discover: white, the lost place.
before, they were led to the roads and now this
passage without bearing, wandering, the loss
that threatens their dreams. according to re-
ports: they believed they had gone the length
of the valleys in their escape, fleeing or devastated by doubt, having fallen into fast water,
shattered in narrow passes. others repeated
these narrations, made false writings circular.
this dead presence surprising now, growing,
multiplying in its last silent meeting, displacing itself without sound, trampling the
poor grass.
only their short breaths, AH, AH, AH
exhaling sickness
(that skin of another skin brushing all the torn ponchos)

THEY WERE PHOTOGRAPHED FROM THE AIR TO LOCATE
THEIR SANCTUARIES -   TO KNOW WHERE TO SHOOT-

he identifies his own naked suffering figure,
on the white cube where he lies, vertical,
pierced by lights and shadows, silent, in
the oblivion of that bed
                -he thought he was a saint-

pero ya viene este otro de pie
a cortar en dos el hilo
y viene de atrás, así, solo, de las sombras
con su mejor cara

RATATA - TA - TA - RATATATATA
(no te dice nada más)

el cubo ahora se triza en una escena de gri-
to - círculos concéntricos se expanden sal-
picando las paredes blancas - el audio si-
gue persiguiendo al caído emisor descontro-
lado que en sombras aún no lo oye, sólo oye
los siguientes golpes - percusión tribal -
en su cabeza, y alcanza a esconder la cara
(recuerda el sol en las dunas, donde juncos
movidos por el viento cantan para él)
mira al otro y no espera nada de su mirada
perdida

RATATA - TA - TA - RATATATATA

me acerqué a sus restos y le susurré al
oído algunas palabras sueltas, vaguedades
sin hilo (ya no me oye) luego soplé con dis-
tintas intensidades
imité al viento para él
imité a las arenas
imité a los juncos
lo imité a él mismo

LAS MANCHAS SE DESLIZABAN
DE ARRIBA ABAJO EN SILENCIO

tiñeron los grandes planos de papel col-gante, blancos vendajes,
ondeando sobre los obscuros rincones de la pintura inte-rior, donde
pintan de leche también sus extremidades, goteantes, danzan y las
albas orillas de río embaldosado reciben gotas de blanco seminal de lo
que viene (arrastradas por la carne de cuerpos que flotan). el papel de
la piel multiplicado de manchas, recorrido por blanco ama-rillo,
blanco azulado, aplastado hueso sobre cenizas, polvo sobre polvo, la
blan-ca tela surcada por islotes que van que-dando en la retorcida, el
sueño, la utopía

- yacer en la blancura -

but now this other is coming on foot
to cut the thread in two
and he's coming from behind, like this, alone,
from the shadows putting his best foot forward.

RATATA - TA - TA - RATATATATA
(that's all he says to you)

the cube now is shattered into a scene of
screaming - concentric circles expand
spattering the white walls - the audio
keeps on pursuing the fallen uncontrolled
transmitter which in shadows still doesn't
hear him, only hearing the successive blows
- tribal percussion -   against his head, and
he manages to hide his face (he remembers
the sun on the dunes, where the grass sang
for him moved by the wind)   he looks at
the other and expects nothing from his   lost gaze

RATATA - TA - TA - RATATATATA

I came closer to his remains and whispered
a few words in his ear, vague things with
no thread between them (he no longer hears me)
then I blew with different intensities
I imitated the wind for him
I imitated the sands
I imitated the grass
I imitated him

THE STAINS SLID FROM TOP TO BOTTOM IN SILENCE

they stained the great planes of hanging paper, white bandages,
flapping over the dark corners of the painting within, where they
paint with milk as well their extremities, dripping, dancing and the
bleached banks of the tiled river receive drops of seminal whiteness
from whatever passes (drops dragged by the flesh of floating bodies).
the paper of the skin where stains multiply, gone over with yellow-
white, blue-white, crushed bone on ash, dust on dust, the white
canvas furrowed by small islands that remain in the twisting, the
dream, the utopia

- to lie in the whiteness -

ABANDONÓ SU CUERPO AL COLOR

alejada de los centros de la acción pudo ver el fulgor de las hogueras,
como la hoguera de su carne desplazándose de punto en punto - ese
fuego redentor - florecido el territorio de su cuerpo, saltó los límites
en esa fiesta roja, quedando a disposición del desorden: hueco el que
antes volumen, allí fué volteada, deshecha, la arrastraron a adorar
ídolos a besarlos arrodillada, y llorando abrazados los barriobajeros
leyeron en la historia de ese cuerpo obsequiado, su propio porvenir:
ella desbordó la piel y el marco. ríos de lava desenfrenados a esa hora,
bajaron de sus hoyos atravesados de jóvenes cuerpos combatientes y
pintada la cara, pintadas las manos no hubo identidad que la
contuviera: dejó que su carne tomara la forma de turno

- han derramado sobre mí, pues soy su mejor bandera -

TODO ÉL, LA FILIGRANA AZUL DE LA MIRADA

en el otro momento de su avance se cierran tras él, las puertas, las
mismas aguas que se abrieran a su impulso en sueños. una forma de
avanzar que borra su rastro. dice: quemar etapas
sólo resta la débil sombra, la espuma del roce, no voltea, dirige la
mirada al fondo y se niega a la salvación impávido en la textura ahora
de su cara muerta. y desde la profundidad obscura emergen sus
últimas palabras - cadáveres esas fonologías repetidas - a la exterioridad
del brillo solar que las reconstruye y recuerda desde ellas la
configuración de sus labios, sin freno ni aliento

- perdí toda distancia -

SHE ABANDONED HER BODY TO THE COLOR

distant from the centers of the action, she could see the brilliance of the bonfires, like the bonfire of her flesh displacing itself from point to point - that redeeming fire - the territory of her body in bloom, she leaped beyond limits into that red festival, remaining at the disposition of the disorder: hollow what once was volume, there she was tipped over, undone, they dragged her to adore idols, to kiss them on her knees, and crying as they embraced each other the people of the lower class read in the history of that body given them, their own future: she overflowed the skin and the frame. rivers of unleashed lava at that time came down from their holes crossed by the bodies of young combatants and with her painted face and painted hands there was no identity that could contain her: she let her flesh take the successive shapes.

- they have spilled over me, since I am their best flag -

ALL OF HIM, THE BLUE FILIGREE OF THE GAZE

in the other moment of his advance the doors close behind him, the same waters that opened on impulse in his dreams. a way of advancing that erases his trail. he says: to burn phases
all that is left is the weak shadow, the foam of contact, he does not topple, he directs the gaze to the bottom and denies himself the salvation, without fear, in the texture now of his dead face. and from the deep darkness emerge his last words - cadavers these repeated phonologies - to the exteriority of solar brilliance that rebuilds them and remembers from them the configuration of his lips, with neither bridle nor breath

- I lost all distance -

(   ) mi aparición allí no es
más accidental ni más necesaria
que la de esa columna tras la cual
sólo puedo apoyarme para mirar
la escena y donde reconozco que
es la que cruza mis ojos dándoles
una interrupción blanca en su
lectura
         - verticalidad -
sé que la acaricio como a un gran
falo cuya materia no es sino el
hueco que la llena, derramando a
su vez sobre el campo la sombra
negra que se deja caer sobre unos
activos trabajadores de la letra
como materia de su producción
        y si miro atrás a lo largo de
ese surco de mi memoria vienen a
reunirse como furiosos combatientes a sus bordes, los recuerdos
del nacimiento, de la narración
doblada que ella emite - desde su
interior - desde su aire que sin
boca, fruto de una grabación
doble, deja escapar relatos, miles
de relatos multiplicados y
anudados en una memoria del
país donde todos somos los hijos
perdidos. pues ella nos mira desde
lo alto y sólo a su sombra es
posible desarrollar aún alguna
otra práctica de tachadura o de
resistencia

allí perdimos el nombre y
la cara pues la mano vertiginosa
en trabajar, perdiéndose entre las
carnes de los otros, logró el
conjunto que se visualizó como
una gran pose escondida, que
fuera derramando el hilo de una
repetición sin fin.
    como si toda la GRABACIÓN hubiese
sido desmantelada de sus circuitos
para seguir circulando eterna-
mente, perdiendo su doble lugar
para subdividirse en miles de
fragmentos o en una partidura
que ya no sólo divide el uno del
otro. no sólo da el 1 y 2 sino que
productiva como separación,
impide para siempre que se
constituya ni el 1 ni el 0 ni el
silencio, puesto que subdividiendo
continuamente siempre es la mitad
de la mitad anterior. la cortadura
del corte. el doble del doblez para
siempre desenfrenado, así como
una letra que avanza desapare-
ciendo siempre y sin embargo en
su movimiento - resto de un
relato a su vez para siempre
subdividido - desde todas las caras
de su volumen, desde su pasado y
su presente, desde su antes y su
atrás, es la única certeza material
de lo perdido.

(   )my apparition there is no
more an accident, no more neces-
sary than that of the column
behind which I can only support
myself to look at the scene and
where I recognize that it's what
crosses my eyes giving them a
white interruption in its lecture
- verticality -
I know that I caress it as I would a
great phallus whose matter is
nothing but the hollow that fills
it, spilling the black shadow at
the same time over the field so
that it falls over some active
workers of the letter as matter of
their production
        and if I look behind me the
length of that furrow of my
memory, images of birth gather
like furious combatants along its
edges, images of the folded narra-
tion that she emits - from her
interior - from her air that,
mouthless, fruit of a double
recording, lets stories escape,
thousands of stories multiplying
and knotted in a memory of the
country where we are all the lost
children. because she looks at
us from a high place and only her
shadow can still be developed,
some other practice of deletion or
resistance

there we lost the name and
the face since the dizzying hand
in working, losing itself in the
flesh of the others, achieved the
whole that was visualized as a
great hidden pose that was spilling
the thread of an endless repetition.
as if the entire RECORDING had
been dismantled from its circuits
in order to continue circling
eternally, losing its double place
to subdivide itself into thousands
of fragments or into a part that
no longer just divides the one
from the other. it doesn't just
create 1 and 2 but is productive as
separation, impeding forever that
1 or 0 or silence are constituted,
in that by subdividing contin-
uously it is always the half of the
previous half. the cleavage of
the cut. the double of the fold
forever unleashed, like a letter
always disappearing as it advances
and nevertheless in its movement
- what remains of a story forever
subdivided - from all the faces of
its volume, from its past and its
present, from its before and its
ago, it is the only material certainty
of what's lost.

SERGIO MANSILLA
(1958)

Due to its isolated geographical location and strong indigenous culture, the island of Chiloé is still the repository of a rich mythology. It is said that clandestine cells of witches persist even today in some of the more remote areas. The poetry of Sergio Mansilla, who was born and raised in a tiny island village where his parents worked as *campesinos*, is filled with the mythological characters that populated his childhood dreams. The following poems contain references to the deformed sailors who live in the phantom ship called *El Caleuche* and also to *la voladora*, the woman who vomits her intestines and transforms herself into a bird *(la bauda)* so she can carry messages for the witches. The landscape of Chiloé—the sea, the forests, the rain and wind, and the green rolling hills planted with potatoes—is a key element in Mansilla's poetry. Sergio Mansilla lives and works as a school teacher in Osorno in southern Chile. He got his start as a poet with the *Aumen* group in Castro, Chiloé.

TIEMPO

*Me parece estar sentado en un cerrito, que la gente llama "altos,"
desde donde se tiene un panorama impresionante: el mar azul, de un
azul desteñido, quieto como una muchedumbre postrada ante un
altar, la costa de la isla cercana casi encima, sus casas nítidas, sus
árboles, sus murras, y hasta se puede ver, aguzando la vista, la gente
que trabaja en la siembra de papas. A la izquierda y lejano, el pueblo
de Curaco de Vélez. Se ven las casas de una blancura apagada aunque
son de diversos colores, y al centro una iglesia nueva por donde pasan
los muertos y los vivos en un camino desconocido. El viento marino
que me enfría el rostro es también la vida; y esta rama de guiacha o de
maqui, y este sol achacoso, y estas calles como ríos secos, y esta gente
como sangre, y este dolorazo feliz que se sienta tras una mesa porque
sí, porque le dio la gana. Esto es también la vida.*

*Tiempo, tiempo de mis pasos y mi carreta,
lleva el nombre de esta amplitud bulliciosa del mar
a la única morada de los mortales;
oculta estos oscuros trenes sin pasajeros
sin pueblos, sin conductor,
como un pájaro ciego sin viento
a través de los días y los ríos errantes
de la tierra de Chiloé.
Y nos vendrá el mar como un perro de agua
a echarse a nuestros pies,
y nos mirará soñoliento
con sus ojos llenos de barcos y marineros
que echan a flamear sus almas como banderas.
Nos vendrá un pan el hombro.
Nos vendrán cánticos de gente dura
en la que anidan los pájaros.
Tiempo, tiempo,
estás en la puerta definitivamente
sentado debajo de mi poncho
mirando el invierno que viene quebrando los cristales
con su bastón de ciego resentido.*

TIME

I imagine myself sitting on one of those hills people call "high places" where there's an impressive view: the blue sea, a faded blue, quiet like a crowd kneeling before an altar, the coast of the nearby island almost on top of me, its neat houses, its trees, its blackberry bushes, and as far one can see, looking very closely, the people who are planting potatoes. To the left, in the distance, the town called Curaco de Vélez. You can see the houses and their dull whiteness even though they are different colors. And in the center, there's a new church where the dead and the living pass by on an unknown road. The sea wind that blows cold against my face is also life; and this branch of *quiacha* or *maqui*, and this ailing sun, and these streets like dry rivers, and these people like blood, and this great pain that sits down happily at a table just because, just because it felt like it. This is also life.

> Time, time of my footsteps and my cart,
> carry the name of this noisy breadth of the sea
> to the only home of the mortals;
> hide these dark trains without passengers
> villages or conductors,
> like a blind bird without wind
> through the days and the wandering rivers
> of the land of Chiloé.
> And the sea will come to us like a dog of water
> to throw itself at our feet
> and will look at us with its sleepy eyes
> filled with ships and sailors
> who hoist their souls like banners.
> A piece of bread on a shoulder will come to us.
> The prayers of hard people where the birds nest
> will come to us.
> Time, time,
> you're in the doorway forever
> sitting beneath my poncho
> watching the winter come to break windows
> like an angry blind man with a cane.

CAUQUIL*

Cauquil, Cauquil.
El mar aúlla en la noche como un lobo hambriento:
Cauquil, Cauquil,
y hay sombras en mi carreta que se aleja
del mundo,
rechinando sobre una playa negra
que amanece corcheteada a un ayer sin terminar.
Y aúlla el mar
y Dios sopla y sopla sobre Cauquil hasta que desordena los años
y se desinfla su cabeza de tanto soplar,
pero Cauquil permanece invariable
como una espada prohibida en medio de un millón de Kilociclos por
                                                            segundo.
En junio,
cuando el invierno es una boca a medio abrir,
Cauquil sube sube
con una lágrima en su motor
a rayar el cielo con un arcoiris.
Pero Cauquil tiene una araña en el fondo de sus ojos,
y yo no tengo tiempo de mirar la hora
y me alejo del mundo
en mi carreta
y Cauquil se va quedando atrás, muy atrás
y me alejo y me alejo
porque mi corazón lo tengo anclado
en la tumba de mi retrato.
Y el mar aúlla en la noche
como si fuera un lobo prisionero en el tiempo.

Al ir caminando sobre las playas barrosas de Chiloé, salta agua con barro y se produce una extraña fosforescencia cuyo color es un verdeazul intenso.

CAUQUIL*

Cauquil, Cauquil.
The sea howls in the night like a hungry wolf:
Cauquil, Cauquil.
And there are shadows in my cart
as it gets farther from the world
and creaks over a black beach
stapled to an endless yesterday at dawn.
And the sea howls
and God blows and blows over Cauquil
scattering the years
until his head collapses from blowing so hard.
But Cauquil remains the same
like a forbidden sword in a million kilocycles per second.
In June,
when winter is a half-open mouth,
Cauquil rises, rises
with a tear in its engine
to line the sky with a rainbow.
But Cauquil has a spider at the bottom of its eyes,
and I don't have time to keep track of the hour
and I get farther from the world
in my cart
and Cauquil remains behind in the distance
and I get farther and farther away
because my heart is anchored
in the tomb of my portrait.
And the sea howls in the night
as if it were a wolf imprisoned in time.

---

*When one walks along the muddy beaches of Chiloé, a mixture of water
and mud spurts to produce a strange phosphorescence that is an intense
blue-green color.

PARTIDA

Cuando los marineros de una-sola-pierna
vinieron a buscarte
dormías en tu cama y soñabas con un inmenso
perro negro que te perseguía por un camino desconocido
ladrando y mordiendo tus talones, haciéndote correr
hasta caer de cansancio sobre un charco de agua roja.
Te despertaron y te dijeron "es la hora, arriba."
Silenciosamente te levantaste, te vestiste
y por el sendero lleno de chucaos
que cantaban a la mano izquierda
llegaste hasta la playa que parecía
iluminada como una ciudad.
Una suave y dulce música acompasada con las olas
hacía ondular los barrancos que se trizaban como vidrios,
y, hechizado, semejante a un grano de sal en una laguna,
te disolviste en la noche misteriosa.

LEAVING

When the one-legged sailors
came to look for you,
you were asleep in your bed, dreaming
about a giant black dog that was chasing you
down an unknown road,
barking and biting your heels, making you run
until you dropped from exhaustion
in a puddle of red water.
They woke you and said, "It's time. Let's go."
You got up in silence, got dressed
and walked down the path
where the *chucaos* sang—but off to your left.
You came to the beach which seemed
lit like a city.
A gentle, sweet music with the rhythm of the waves
made the cliffs sway until they cracked like windows.
And, bewitched, like a grain of salt in a lake,
you dissolved in the mysterious night.

*ATARDECER EN CHANGÜITAD**

*El creciente aire, fino, entre hierbas,
alejado de toda duda posible, infla la blusa
entre sombras de póstumos ganados.
Se oye el mar, lejos, pero lo apaga
el ruido interior que emerge desorbitado
hasta el cielo, cual negra columna de humo.*

*Hora es de recogerse y guardar las herramientas:
pero, semicerrados los ojos
ante el crepitar de luces anodinas,
permanecen inmóviles los sentimientos
y giran sobre sí mismos.*

*La hoz ha segado el eterno instante
del encuentro en paz con el propio destino,
sólo el viento y las primeras estrellas
se instalan en los ojos.*

*Y en mitad del campo, solitaria,
una mujer levanta sus brazos
y vuelan pájaros chillando hacia los ramajes yertos.*

---

*Changüitad es la tierra donde viví mi infancia, en Chiloé.

DUSK IN CHANGÜITAD*

The fine air grows among the grass,
far from any possible doubt, and fills the blouse
among shadows of posthumous cattle.
The sea can be heard in the distance, but
the inner noise that emerges, wildly climbing
to the sky like a column of black smoke, drowns it out.

It's time to go home and put away the tools,
but, with half-closed eyes
before the crackling of unimportant lights,
feelings remain, immobile,
spinning.

The sickle has reaped the eternal instant
of the meeting in peace with one's own fate;
only the wind and the first stars
occupy the eyes.

And in the middle of the field, alone,
a woman lifts her arms
and birds fly, calling to dead branches.

---

*Changüitad is the land where I lived as a boy, in Chiloé.

AMOR

Y la mujer vomitó sus entrañas
y voló en la noche negra hasta la Casa de sus Sueños.
El hombre, recostado en su cama, veía
un pájaro aletear afuera ante su ventana;
se alejaba y volvía otra vez a picotear
con furia los vidrios escarchados.
El hombre trató de dormir, mas esa ave
insistía en la ventana una y otra vez incansable,
hasta que, ciego de ira, se levantó
y salió al patio y cogío una piedra
que arrojó a la cabeza de aquella bauda loca
que se reía en las sombras.
Cuando volvió, estaba blanco,
y al otro día, sin saber por qué, se sintió mejor,
y por la tarde, soltó una carcajada
afirmado en las lajas humedecidas por el mar.

LOVE

And the woman coughed up her entrails
and flew through the night to the House of her Dreams.
The man, lying in his bed, saw
a bird flutter outside at his window;
it flew away and then returned again to peck
furiously at the panes covered with frost.
The man tried to sleep, but that bird
persisted at the window again and again,
until finally, blind with rage, he got up
and went out on the patio and picked up a stone
and threw it at the head of that crazy *bauda*
that laughed in the shadows.
When he went back inside, he was white,
and the next day, without knowing why, he felt better,
and in the afternoon, he broke out laughing
as he leaned against slabs of stone washed by the sea.

ÁNIMAS ERRANTES

Al caer la tarde una multitud de muertos
vuelve a sus casas,
buscan sus tierras y sus hogares
que la memoria les recuerda.

Vuelven, y a cada paso queda
un espacio íntimo vacío
que llenan las estrellas
con brillantes luciérnagas rojas-violetas.

Multitudes de sombras andan
en la noche por los campos
y su paso hace andar los molinos a agua
y quejarse los árboles, como agonizantes
abandonados en hondanadas remotas.

Llegan al umbral de sus casas
y ven la humilde cocina iluminada
por dos toscos chonchones de grasa.

Sus casas están cerradas, como durmiendo,
y alzan la mano para llamar a la puerta.

Al llamado, sale un niño a abrir;
mas, aunque mira atentamente,
no ve a nadie: sólo distingue vagamente
un paisaje solitario donde apenas
se escucha el lejano canto de las aves nocturnas.

WANDERING SOULS

At dusk the multitude of the dead
returns to where it lived.
They look for their lands and homes
that memory brings back.

They return, and at each step
an intimate space empties
and the stars fill it
with violet fireflies of light.

Multitudes of shadows move
through the night across the fields
and their steps make the waterwheels turn
and the trees complain like the dying
abandoned in remote valleys.

They stand at the doorways of their houses
and see the humble kitchens lit
by two crude oil lamps.

Their houses are closed, as if asleep,
and they lift their hands to knock on the door.

When he hears the knocking, a child opens the door.
But even though he keeps staring,
he doesn't see anyone—only a vague
lonely landscape where the distant cry
of night birds can scarcely be heard.

LA VIDA

Esperamos a nuestros muertos incontables años
afirmados en los cercos.
Abrazados a las estacas soportamos los vientos huracanados,
el granizo, la escarcha y los soles
que partían la tierra y llenaban
los palos secos de lagartijas.

Nuestras cabezas de jabón
se disolvían por la nostalgia;
se gastaban nuestros ojos por mirar
tanto los mismos cerros,
los mismos manzanos y los mismos álamos
cimbrados por el viento desatado del noroeste.

Levantamos cuanto pudimos nuestras casas,
juntamos piedras y pies derechos,
tijerales y miles de tejuelas partidas a machetón.
Pero se mutilaron nuestras manos
y huyeron de nuestros brazos como pájaros por los aires
y cuando regresaron ya estábamos ciegos y mudos.
No supimos de nuestro destino
y echamos raíces donde se deposita el cieno del invierno.

Así, de a poco, nos fuimos desnudando de nuestras ropas;
primero de las más gruesas,
luego de nuestra ropa interior,
más tarde nos desprendimos de nuestras carnes y huesos
hasta quedar sólo la transparente y clara esencia
sin forma ni rastro, sin apariencia alguna:
acaso sólo una palabra, sólo la idea pura
de hombre o mujer
en medio del tiempo indescriptible y aullando.

LIFE

We wait for our dead countless years
as we lean against fences.
Embracing the posts we resist hurricane winds,
hail, frost and suns
that split the earth and filled
the dry sticks with lizards.

Our heads of soap
dissolved from so much nostalgia;
our eyes wasted away from looking
so long at the same hills,
the same apple trees and the same poplars
bent by wind unleashed from the northwest.

We raised as many of our houses as we could;
we gathered stones and studs
and rafters and thousands of wooden shingles
split by machete.
But our hands were mutilated
and fled from our arms through the air like birds.
And when they returned, we were already blind and mute.
We had no idea of our destinies
and set down roots in the winter mud.

So, little by little, we began taking off our clothing;
first the heaviest things,
then what we wore underneath,
and later we got rid of our flesh and bones
until all that was left was a clear, transparent essence—
with neither form nor trace nor any appearance at all.
Perhaps just a word, just the pure idea
of man or woman
in the middle of the indescribable and howling time.

MAURICIO ELECTORAT

(1960)

Mauricio Electorat's startling imagery and rigorous use of language are surprising in so young a poet. His poetry is urban and aware: it is difficult to imagine a more chilling poem than "The Slaughterhouse," which describes the institutionalization and mechanization of death in the only system of life the poet has really known in his country. Electorat's elegy, "For Armando Rubio," locates one of the casualties of youth in the environment of Santiago with its lights, asphalt, and street vendors selling peanuts from the city's familiar blue and white carts shaped like boats.

Electorat recently left Chile to continue his studies in Spain.

EL MATADERO

a Cristián Warnken

El trabajo de las sierras separando las vértebras
puede oírse desde afuera como un zumbido sordo y regular,
la bruma cae sobre las bodegas de latón y los callejones sin luz
por donde se deslizan sospechosas sombras.
La exactitud de les sierras separando las cabezas que caen al vacío,
los motores que rechinan como búfalos metálicos -
muy lejos escucho algunos automóviles y ya huelo a los muertos,
a los descuartizados, a los que fueron presos de trampas más sutiles.
La muerte, algo que se ha extraviado en un sórdido callejón de barrio
y más allá
luces de una avenida que se pierde en la bruma roja.

PARA ARMANDO RUBIO

Pasa un barco manicero al final de la calle,
el cielo jacinto recibirá pronto otro sol
y he visto a esta hora híbrida
automóviles llenos de ángeles adentrarse en los bosques
arrastrando colgajos de luces amarillas y rojas
        pero no es eso,
chirrian las latas oxidadas del barco manicero
y al final de la calle
como si hubiese caído sobre una ola de asfalto
el marinero triste yace muerto

THE SLAUGHTERHOUSE

The work of the saws separating the vertebrae
can be heard from outside: a deaf and regular buzzing.
The fog descends on the zinc-roofed stores and lightless alleys
where suspicious shadows slip past.
The exactness of the saws separating the heads that fall in the void,
the motors whining like metallic buffaloes—
far away I hear some cars and already I can smell the dead,
the quartered bodies, the ones that were trapped with subtler tricks.
Death, something that wanders lost in an alley in the bad part of town
and beyond
lights from an avenue that disappears in the red fog.

FOR ARMANDO RUBIO

A boat with a cargo of peanuts passes at the end of the street,
the hyacinth sky will soon receive another sun
and I've seen at this hybrid hour
cars filled with angels entering the woods
dragging strings of red and yellow lights
        but it's not that,
the rusty cans of the boat with a cargo of peanuts hiss
and at the end of the street
as if he had fallen on a wave of asphalt,
the sad sailor lies dead.

CIUDAD SATÉLITE

Un vasto espacio de tierra seca
alrededor de las rejas que rodean estos cubos de cemento
El horizonte es una nube de polvo
que se pierde en las montañas, pálidas colinas de sal
Encima cuelga siempre el sol, ese escarabajo rojo y ancho
y los hombres están todo el día encerrados en sus cubos calientes,
huesos blancos son la única cosecha en estas arenas amarillas

TODA LA NOCHE EN TREN, TODA LA NOCHE

Toda la noche el tren
desplazándose como una oruga lenta
entre las luces de un caserío y otro
avanzando hacia atrás hacia adelante
sobre las aguas congeladas del lago
sobre los campos lisos y estirados de la nieve
hacia atrás hacia adelante
sobre los campos muertos de la nieve
mientras tratamos de dormir
entre los sacos con frutas
los sacos con yerbas
y el hedor de los hombres
que duermen echados
en el pasillo
toda la noche
como gallinas
quietos

SATELLITE CITY

A vast space of dry land
surrounds the bars of these cement cubes
The horizon is a cloud of dust
disappearing in the mountains, pale hills of salt
The sun is always hanging above: that wide, red beetle
and the men spend all day enclosed in their hot cubes,
white bones are the only harvest on these yellow sands

ALL NIGHT LONG BY TRAIN, ALL NIGHT LONG

All night long the train
crawling like a slow caterpillar
among the lights of one tiny village after another
advancing backwards and forwards
over the frozen waters of the lake
over the smooth, stretching fields of snow
backwards and forwards
over the dead fields of snow
while we try to sleep
among sacks of fruit
sacks of herbs
and the stench of men
sleeping sprawled
in the corridor
all night long
like still hens

EL RETORNO

¿Qué es esto
de volver a los mismos lugares?
Las nubes
          hongos grises
                    hongos negros
siempre se arremolinan antes de la tormenta
y se derrumba el agua
fresca como el resuello de los dioses
- y el polvo de sus huesos
cayendo desde el cielo
se deposita debajo de las piedras.

Toda el agua del mundo,
sobre los campos amarillos de cebada y la infinita
llanura azul del cielo, que llora toda la noche
lloviendo sobre la interminable huella
de mis huesos.

THE RETURN

What's all this
about returning to the same places?
The clouds
        gray mushrooms
                black mushrooms
they always swirl before the storm
and the water pours down,
fresh like the breath of the gods—
and the dust of their bones
falling from the sky
is deposited beneath the stones.
All the water of the world
over the yellow fields of grain and the infinite
blue plain of the sky, that cries all night
raining on the interminable trail
of my bones.

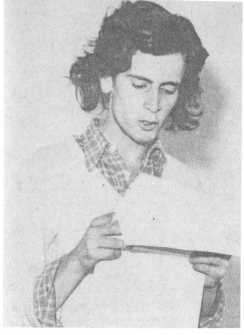

IN MEMORY OF

Rodrigo Lira (1949-1981)

Armando Rubio (1955-1980)

Numerous poets in Chile have died at an early age, leaving behind a sheaf of manuscripts: Domingo Gómez Rojas, Romeo Murga, Jorge Cáceres, Alberto Rojas Jiménez, Joaquín Cifuentes Sepúlveda, Boris Calderón, Gustavo Ossorio and, now, Rodrigo Lira and Armando Rubio. The violent suicide of Lira and Rubio's accidental death after falling from a balcony produced the inevitable trail of elegies in the tradition of poems such as Pablo Neruda's "Alberto Rojas Jiménez viene volando" and "Una vez el azar se llamó Jorge Cáceres" by Gonzalo Rojas. "Ars Poetique" by Rodrigo Lira is a polemical, satiric attack on some great figures of Chilean poetry who have written on the same subject: Huidobro, Neruda, Parra, Lihn. Armando Rubio's self-portrait in "Anonymous Biography" is a last will and testament of an alienated, bohemian life in an urban context.

ARS POETIQUE

Para la galería imaginaria

Que el verso sea como una ganzúa
Para entrar a robar de noche
Al diccionario a la luz
De una linterna sorda como
Tapia,
    muro de los lamentos,
¡Pared de oídos!

Cae un rocket, *pasa un* Mirage:
Los ventanales quedaron temblando.

Estamos en el siglo de las neuras y las siglas.
El músculo se vende por correo, la ambición
No descansa La Poesía
Está colgando en la Dirección
De Bibliotecas, Archivos y Museos, en Artículos
De lujo, de primera
Necesidad
    ¡Oh Poetas!
No cantéis a las rosas, hacedlas
Mermelada de mosqueta en el poema.

Porque escribo estoy así. Por
Que escribí porque escribí "estoy vivo";
La Poesía terminó conmigo: huero, vacuo, gastado
E inútil *ejercicio (el adjetivo mata, mata:)*
Frivolidad ociosa, tediosa y
Esporádica.
    Cuando escriba, no conduzca.

Sólo para nosotros mueren todas las cosas
Bajo el sol:
    Nada nuevo:
        Decadentismo de primera

ARS POETIQUE

for the *imaginary gallery*

Let poetry be like a skeleton key
To enter and steal the dictionary
At night by the light
Of a lantern deaf as an
Adobe wall,
        wailing wall,
Wall of ears!

A rocket falls, a *Mirage* goes by:
The windows shake.

We're in the century of neuroses and acronyms.
Muscles are sold by mail, ambition
Never rests Poetry
Is hanging in the Head Offices
Of Libraries, Archives and Museums,
From items of luxury, from things of basic
Need
        Oh Poets!
Don't just sing the roses, make them
Rose marmalade in the poem.

Because I write, I'm like this. Be
Cause I wrote because I wrote "I'm alive";
Poetry ended with me: vain, empty, worn out
And *useless* exercise (the adjective kills, it kills:)
Lazy, tedious and sporadic
Frivolity.
        When you write, don't drive.

Only for us does everything under the sun
die:
    Nothing new:
        First class decadence

Mano, a mano hemos quedado los poetas
Son unos pequeñísimos
Reptiles: ni alquimistas ni albañiles ni
Andinistas: bajaron del olimpo y
Se sacaron la cresta. Palabras
En la noche ya nada está en calma.
                    Poetry
May be Hazardous to your Health.*
-Se va ella o me voy yo . . .!   *-Oh Poesía . . .*
. . . nuestro ayuntamiento
                              . . . acaba/

—————————————————
*La Poesía puede ser riesgosa para s(t)u salud.

We poets are on equal terms now.
You're just a bunch of tiny
Reptiles: not alchemists or bricklayers or
Mountain climbers: you came down from Olympus
and got the shit beat out of you. Words
In the night, nothing is calm anymore.
                        Poetry
May be Hazardous to your Health.
—Either she goes or I go . . .!—Oh Poetry . . .
 . . . our relationship
                        . . . is over/

BIOGRAFÍA ANÓNIMA

Soy un oscuro ciudadano
abandonado en medio de las calles
por el cuchillo sin pan del mediodía,
despojado y marchito
como el reloj de las iglesias,
sin otro oficio que vagar entre disfraces.

Soy el familiar venido a menos,
enraizado a las tabernas
y a la complicidad del bandolero.
Mi voz naufraga en los cristales de las tiendas,
y he perdido la vista en los periódicos,
pero tengo los pies bien puestos sobre la tierra
y una almohada que vuela por los hospitales
y por los dormitorios del oscuro hogar de nadie.
Tengo una celda amable en las comisarías,
y suelo bailar a hurtadillas bajo la noche
con mi camisa blanca
y mi corbata deshojada.

Soy un oscuro ciudadano
extraviado por el mundo:
voy cogiendo colillas de cigarros,
y canto en los tranvías,
y me peino hacia atrás, valientemente,
para mostrar mi noble frente anónima
en los baños públicos y en los circos de mi barrio.

Soy un oscuro habitante: no soy nadie;
en nada me distingo de algún otro ciudadano;
tengo abuelas y parientes que se han ido
y una espalda ancha que socava
la pared amiga de las cervecerías.

ANONYMOUS BIOGRAPHY

I'm a dark citizen
abandoned in the middle of the streets
by the knife without bread at noon,
homeless and withering away
like the steeple clocks,
with no other job except to wander among disguises.

I'm the relative in decline,
rooted in the taverns
and the complicity of thieves.
My voice shipwrecks on store windows,
and I've lost my sight in the newspapers.
But I have my feet firmly planted on the earth
and a pillow that flies through hospitals
and rooms in the dark home that belongs to no one.
I've got a nice cell in the police stations
and I'm used to dancing in secret beneath the night
with my white shirt
and my tie stripped of its leaves.

I'm a dark citizen
misplaced by the world:
I pick up cigarette butts
and sing in the streetcars,
and I comb back my hair, valiantly,
to show my noble anonymous forehead
in the public bathrooms and circuses where I live.

I'm a dark citizen; I'm no one;
nothing distinguishes me from some other citizen;
I have grandmothers and relatives who've gone away
and a wide back digging
under the friendly walls of the beer halls.

Soy una ola entre todas las olas,
una ola que se levanta
a las seis de la mañana
porque ya no puede
oler el polvo de su casa,
una ola que se alza, alborozada
hacia las playas
para un retorno interminable al centro de las cosas
donde las olas todas
se empujan mutuamente
estériles y solas.

Porque yo no soy digno de mi semen,
Señor, yo no soy nada;
estoy en medio de las calles
girando como un organillero
con mi camisa gastada, inamovible,
mirándome la punta del zapato
por si alguien quiere darme
una moneda que no quiero,
aunque nadie me ha visto pasar
esta tarde ni nunca,
porque nunca soy alguien,
ni siquiera un oscuro ciudadano
resucitado por el hambre.

Mi voz ha muerto en los cristales de las tiendas,
y tengo una espuma de mar aquí en la boca, ebrio,
porque soy una ola entre todas las olas,
que viene a morir en esta arena de miseria
decentemente con su traje de franela
y su ciega corbata
como buen hombre que era.

Fui un oscuro ciudadano,
Señor, no lo divulgues,
cesante, ¡sí!
Hasta aquí llegó la vida,
pero recuerda al fin:
yo nunca pedí nada
porque tuve camisa blanca.

I'm a wave among all the waves,
a wave that rises
at six in the morning
because it can no longer
smell the dust in its house,
a wave, lifting itself, filled with joy,
toward the beaches
for an endless return to the center of things
where all the waves
push each other—
sterile and alone.

Because I am not worthy of my semen,
Lord, I'm nothing;
I'm in the middle of the streets
spinning like an organ grinder
with my worn, immovable shirt,
watching the tips of my shoes
in case someone wants to give me
a coin I don't want,
even though no one has seen me go by
this afternoon or ever,
because I'm never anyone,
not even a dark citizen
brought back to life by hunger.

My voice has died in the store windows,
and my mouth is filled with surf, I'm drunk,
because I'm a wave among all the waves,
who comes to die on this sand of misery,
decently, with a flannel suit
and a blind tie
like the good man I was.

I was once a dark citizen,
Lord, don't tell anyone,
and unemployed, that's right!
So, this is where life ends up,
but remember after all:
I never asked for anything
because I had a white shirt.

SELECTIVE BIBLIOGRAPHY

Calderón, Teresa. *Causas perdidas*. Santiago: Ediciones Artesanales, 1984.

Cameron, Juan. *Las manos enlazadas*. Valparaíso: Edeval, 1971.

—— *Una vieja joven muerte*. Valparaíso: n.p., 1972.

—— *Perro de circo*. Santiago: n.p., 1979.

—— *Apuntes*. Valparaíso: Ediciones del Café, 1981.

—— *Escrito en Valparaíso*. Santiago: Gráfica Marginal, 1982.

—— &. Viña del Mar: Ediciones del Café, 1984.

Electorat, Mauricio. *Un buey sobre mi lengua*. Unpublished.

España, Aristóteles. *La guitarra de mis sueños*. Punta Arenas: n.p., 1972; rpt. Punta Arenas: n.p., 1976.

—— *Incendio en el silencio*. Punta Arenas: n.p., 1978.

—— *Equilibrios e incomunicaciones*. Punta Arenas: n.p., 1975, rpt. Punta Arenas: n.p., 1980 and Santiago: n.p., 1982.

Hahn, Oscar. *Esta rosa negra*. Santiago: Editorial Universitaria, 1961.

—— *Agua final*. Lima: Ediciones de la Rama Florida, 1967.

—— *Arte de morir*. Buenos Aires: Hispamérica, 1977; rpt. Santiago: Nascimento, 1979; and Lima: Ruray, 1981.

—— *Mal de amor*. Santiago: Ediciones Ganymedes, 1981.

——. *Imágenes nucleares*. Santiago: Editorial América del Sur, 1983.

Hoefler, Walter. *Dos cantos (voces y resonancias)*. Valdivia: Universidad Austral, 1970.

——. *Segunda expulsión del paraíso (oct.-nov. 1973)*. *Proposiciones* (Santiago: Sur) 3, No. 9 (1983): pp. 19-37.

——. "Bajo ciertas circunstancias." *El Correo de Valdivia*, 9-II-1978, n.p.

Lara, Omar. *Argumento de día*. Cautín: Imprenta "Padre las Casas," 1964.

——. *Los enemigos*. Santiago-Valdivia: Ediciones Mimbre, 1967.

——. *Los buenos días*. Valdivia: Ediciones de Poesía Trilce, 1972.

——. *Serpientes*. (Lima, 1974).

——. *Oh buenas maneras*. Havana: Premio Casa de las Américas, 1975.

——. *Crónica del reyno de Chile*. (1976).

——. *El viajero imperfecto*. (1979).

——. *Islas flotantes*. Bilingual, translated by Mihai Cantuniari. Bucharest: Carta Románeasca, 1980.

——. *Fugar con juego*. Madrid: Ediciones LAR, 1984.

Lira, Rodrigo. *Proyecto de obras completas*. Santiago: Coedición Minga-Camaleón, 1984.

Mansilla, Sergio. *El viajero de los días extraños*. Unpublished.

Maquieira, Diego. *Upsilon*. Santiago: Printer Ltda., 1975.

———. *Bombardo*. Santiago: Laboratorio Fotográfico, 1977.

———. *La tirana*. Santiago: Edición Tempus Tacendi, 1983.

Martínez, Juan Luis. *La nueva novela*. Santiago: Ediciones Archivo, 1977.

———. *La poesía chilena*. Santiago: Ediciones Archivo, 1978.

Millán, Gonzalo. *Relación personal*. Santiago: Arancibia Hermanos, 1968.

———. *La ciudad*. Quebec: Les editions Maison Culturelle Québec-Amérique Latine, 1979.

———. *Seudónimos de la muerte*. Santiago: Ediciones Manieristas, 1984.

———. *Vida 1968-1982*. Ottawa: Ediciones Cordillera, 1984.

Molina, Paz. *Memorias de un pájaro asustado*. Santiago: Impreso por Editorial Universitaria, 1982.

———. *Cosas de ciegos*. Unpublished.

Muñoz, Gonzalo. *Exit*. Santiago: Ediciones Archivo, 1981.

———. *Este*. Santiago: Impreso en Talleres de la Editorial Universitaria, 1984.

Quezada, Jaime. *Poemas de las cosas olvidadas*. Santiago: Orfeo, 1965.

———. *Las palabras del fabulador*. Santiago: Editorial Universitaria, 1968.

———. *Astrolabio*. Santiago: Nascimento, 1976.

———. *Huerfanías*. Unpublished.

Riedemann, Clemente. *Karra maw'n*. Valdivia: Ediciones Alborada, 1984.

Rojas, Waldo. *Agua removida*. (1964).

———. *Príncipe de naipes*. (1966).

———. *Cielorraso*. Santiago: Ediciones Letras, Colección el Basilisco, 1971.

———. *El puente oculto*. Madrid: Ediciones Literatura Americana Reunida, 1981.

———. *Almenara*. Unpublished.

Rubio, Armando. *Ciudadano*. Santiago: Ediciones Minga, 1983.

Silva Acevedo, Manuel. *Perturbaciones*. Santiago: Ediciones Renovación, 1967.

———. *Lobos y ovejas*. Santiago: Edición de la Galería Paulina Waugh, 1976.

———. *Mester de bastardía*. Santiago: Ediciones El Viento en la Llama, 1977.

———. *Monte de Venus*. Santiago: Editorial del Pacífico, 1979.

———. *Terrores diurnos*. Santiago: n.p., 1982.

Zurita, Raúl. *Purgatorio*. Santiago: Editorial Universitaria, 1979.

———. *Anteparaíso*. Santiago: Editores Asociados, 1982.

Useful Anthologies

(Chronological Order)

Poesía chilena, 1960-1965. Ed. Omar Lara and Carlos Cortínez. Santiago: Editorial Universitaria, 1966.

Antología de la poesía chilena contemporánea. Ed. Alfonso Calderón. Santiago: Editorial Universitaria, 1970.

10 años de poesía joven en Chile. Valparaíso: Universidad de Chile de Valparaíso, 1971.

Nueva poesía joven en Chile. Ed. Martín Micharvegas. Buenos Aires: Ediciones Noé, 1972.

Poesía joven de Chile. Ed. Jaime Quezada. Mexico: Siglo Veintiuno, 1973.

Poesía femenina chilena. Ed. Nina Donoso. Santiago: Editora Nacional Gabriela Mistral, 1974.

"Selección de poesía: 1961-1973." Ed. Oscar Hahn and Waldo Rojas. *Hispamérica* 9 (1975): pp. 55-71.

Poesía para el camino. Santiago: Ediciones Nueva Universidad, 1977.

Los poetas chilenos luchan contra el fascismo. Ed. Sergio Macías. Berlin, East Germany: Comité Chileno Antifascista, 1977.

Chile: poesía de las cárceles y del destierro. Madrid: Ediciones Conosur, 1978.

Chile: poesía de la resistencia y del exilio. Ed. Omar Lara and Juan Epple. Bucharest: n.p., 1978.

Poesía joven del sur de Chile. Ed. Osvaldo Rodriguez. Valdivia: Universidad Austral, 1978.

"Poetas de la generación disgregada violentada." *La Bicicleta* (Santiago) 5 (1979): pp. 11-15.

Uno x uno, algunos poetas jóvenes. Santiago: Editorial Nascimento, 1979.

Ganymedes 6. Ed. David Turkeltaub. Santiago: Ediciones Ganymedes, 1980.

Review 27. Ed. Ronald Christ. New York: Center for Inter-American Relations, 1980.

Ejercicio en sol. Ed. Miguel Arteche. Santiago: Taller Nueve, 1980.

Chilean Literature in Canada. Ed. Naín Nómez. Ottawa: Ediciones Cordillera, 1982.

Entre la lluvia y el arcoiris: Antología de jóvenes poetas chilenos. Ed. Soledad Bianchi. Holland: Ediciones del Instituto para el Nuevo Chile, 1983.

Diez poetas chilenos. Ed. Enrique Moro. Frankfurt: Zambon Verlag, 1983.

"Muestra de nueva poesía chilena." *Literatura chilena, creación y crítica*, No. 26 (1983): pp. 17-22.

"Ocho jovenes poetas chilenos." *Casa de las Américas* 139 (julio-agosto, 1983): pp. 89-99. Based on the anthology edited by Soledad Bianchi. *Poesía chilena contemporánea.* Ed. Miguel Arteche, J. Massone, Roque Esteban Escarpa. Santiago: Andrés Bello, 1984.

"Diez años de poesía." *Solidaridad*: 173-178 (marzo-junio, 1984) (separatas).

Useful Magazines

*no longer published

ALTA MAREA (Santiago)

ARAUCARIA (Madrid)

ARCHIPIELAGO (Ancud)

EL ARBOL (Santiago)

*ARUSPICE (Concepción)

ATENEA (Concepción)

AUMEN (Castro)

EL BARCO DE PAPEL (Paris)

LA BICICLETA (Santiago)

BOLETIN BIBLIOGRAFICO LITERARIO (Santiago)

BUSQUEDA (Puerto Montt)

CABALLO DE PROA (Valdivia)

LA CASTAÑA (Santiago)

EL 100PIES (Santiago)

CONTRAMURO (Santiago)

*ENVES (Concepción)
*ESPIGA (Temuco)
ESPIRITU DEL VALLE (Santiago)
FRAGUA (San Fernando)
*FUEGO NEGRO (Concepción)
LA GOTA PURA (Santiago)
HOJA X OJO (Santiago)
HUELEN (Santiago)
INDICE (Valdivia)
LAR (Madrid)
LATRODECTUS (Temuco)
LITERATURA CHILENA (EN EL EXILIO) (Los Angeles, CA)
*MOMENTOS (Punta Arenas)
NUEVA LINEA (Santiago)
*ORFEO (Santiago)
LA ORUGA (Santiago)
PAJARO DE PAPEL (La Serena)
PALABRA ESCRITA (Santiago)
*PAZQUIN (Santiago)
PLUMA Y PINCEL (Santiago)
POESIA DIARIA (Temuco)
POESIA LIBRE (Coyhaique)
*POLIGONO (Puerto Montt)
PORTAL (Santiago)
POSDATA (Concepción)
*LA QUINTA RUEDA (Santiago)
RECITAL (Antofagasta)
REVISTA CHILENA DE LITERATURA (Santiago)
RIBERA NORTE (Santiago)
RUPTURA - C.A.D.A. (Santiago)
LA SEPARATA (Santiago)
*TEBAIDA (Arica)
TRANVIA
TRILCE (Valdivia-Madrid)

Useful Studies
(criticism on individual poets)

TERESA CALDERÓN

Quezada, Jaime. "Teresa Calderón: *Causas perdidas.*" *Paula* (Santiago) 433 (7-VIII-1984).

Rivera Vivencio, Roberto. "Poesía en la sospecha." *Las Ultimas Noticias* (Santiago) (5-VIII-1984).

JUAN CAMERON

"Juan Cameron: se reconoce vanidoso y le gustaría ser poeta maldito." *La Estrella* (Valparaíso) (1-X-1980) p. 24.

Quezada, Jaime. "Las impertenencias del chambalán." *Ercilla* (Santiago) 2310 (Nov., 1979) pp. 48-49.

OSCAR HAHN

Belli, Carlos Germán. "*Arte de morir.*" *Hispamérica* 18 (1977) pp. 100-101.

Coddou, Marcelo. "*Arte de morir.*" *Revista Iberoamericana* 108-109 (1979) pp. 687-691.

Hill, W. Nick. "Oscar Hahn o el arte de morir." *RCHL* 20 (1982) pp. 99-112.

Lastra, Pedro. "Poesía inédita de Oscar Hahn." *Anales de la Universidad de Chile* 134 (1965) pp. 171-173.

Lihn, Enrique. "Arte del arte de morir." *Texto Crítico* 4 (1976) pp. 47-53.

———. "*Poetas fuera o dentro de Chile 77.*" *Vuelta* 15 (1978) pp. 16-22.

Palau de Nemes, Graciela. "La poesía en movimiento de Oscar Hahn." *Insula* 362 (1977) pp. 10-11.

Rodriguez Padrón, Jorge. "Oscar Hahn: diálogos de la ausencia." *Hora de Poesía* (Barcelona) 21-22 (1982) pp. 44-48.

OMAR LARA

"Omar Lara bajo interrogatorio." *El Siglo* (Santiago) (8-X-1967) p. 16.

Concha, Jaime. "*Los buenos días* de Omar Lara." *El Diario Color* (Concepción) *(8-X-1972) p. 3.

Epple, Juan. "*Crónica del reyno de Chile.*" *Araucaria* 1 (1978) pp. 206-208.

Espinoza Orellana, Manuel. "*Los buenos días.*" *La Nación* (Santiago) (24-XII-1972) p. 14 supl.

Filebo. "Poeta lárico." *Las Ultimas Noticias* (22-VII-1984).

Iñigo Madrigal, Luis. *"Los buenos días* de Omar Lara." *La Nación* (Santiago) (9-VII-1972) p.6.

Puz, Amanda. *"Los buenos días* de Omar Lara." *Paula* 131 (1973) p. 31.

Quezada, Jaime. "Omar Lara: *Fugar con juego."* *Paula* 432 (24-VII-1984) p.95.

Quiñones, Guillermo. "Omar Lara: *Fugar con juego." El Sur* (Concepción) (23-IX-1984) p. II.

Ramirez, Luis Hernán. "La poesía de Omar Lara: nuevo impulso de vida y de combate." *Casa de las Américas* 107 (1978) pp. 72-76.

Round. "Dos poetas perturbados." *Punto Final* (Santiago) 38 (1967) p. 20.

Valente, Ignacio. "Lara y Lastra en sus lares." *El Mercurio* (26-VIII-1984) p. E3.

RODRIGO LIRA

Valente, Ignacio. "Proyecto de Rodrigo Lira." *El Mercurio* (2-XII-1984) p. E3.

DIEGO MAQUIEIRA

Lihn, Enrique. *"La tirana* de Diego Maquieira: un lenguaje violento y 'chilensis'." *Apsi* (Santiago) Feb. 21-March 5 (1984) pp. 34-35.

Marchant, Jorge. *"La tirana." La Segunda* (Santiago) (24-II-1984) p. 32.

Novoa, Mariana. "Un poeta de *Shock." Paula* (Santiago) 426 (2-V-1984) pp. 87-90.

Valdés, Adriana. "Tres poetas de aquí, de ahora y un texto de Adriana Valdés." *La Separata* (Santiago) 5 (1982) pp. 4-5.

JUAN LUIS MARTÍNEZ

Cerda, Martín. "Martínez." *Ultimas Noticias* (Santiago) (13-I-1979) p. 5.

Quezada, Jaime. "Juan Luis Martínez: el desorden de los sentidos." *Ercilla* 2008 (23-XI-1977).

_____. "El libro de las defunciones." *Ercilla* 2274 (28-II-1979) pp. 45-46.

Sánchez de la Torre, Luis. *"La nueva novela." Ultimas Noticias* (Santiago) (26-XI-1977) p. 7.

Valente, Ignacio. "La poesía experimental de J.L. Martínez." *El Mercurio* (20-XI-1977) p. III.

GONZALO MILLÁN

Concha, Jaime. "Exilio, conciencia; coda sobre la poesía de Millán." *Maize* (San Diego, CA) 5, Nos. 1-2 (1981-82) pp. 7-15.

Etcheverry, Jorge. *"Seudónimos de la muerte." Literatura Chilena (creación y crítica)* 30 (otoño, 1984) p. 34.

Filebo. "Libros para el mundo." *Las Ultimas Noticias* (Santiago) (8-IV-1984) p. 14.

Foxley, Ana María. "Seudónimos de la vida." *Hoy* 381 (Nov. 1984) pp. 32-34.

Martínez, Pacián. "Realidades nuevas." *La Gaceta del Bíobío, El Sur* (Concepción) (6-V-1984) pp. 4-5.

Quezada, Jaime. "El recurso del silabario." *Ercilla* 2321 (23-I-1980).

———. "Con la vida en limpio." *Ercilla* (9-V-1984) pp. 42-43.

Pérez, Floridor. "El regreso de un 'hombre extraordinario'." *El Sur* (Concepción) (29-IV-1984).

Rojas, Waldo. "La poesía de Gonzalo Millán." *Punto Final* 57 (1968) pp. 20-21.

Rojo, Grinor. "Poesía chilena del exilio: A propósito de *La ciudad* de Gonzalo Millán." *Ideologies & Literature* 17 (Sept.-Oct., 1983) pp. 256-278.

Skármeta, Antonio. "*Relación personal*." *Revista Chilena de Literatura* 1 (1970) pp. 91-95.

Ulibarri, Luisa. "Gonzalo Millán: en la mitad de mi vida." *Apsi* (8-21-V-1984) pp. 42-43.

Valente, Ignacio. "Dos poetas del exilio." *El Mercurio* (4-V-1980) p. E 3.

White, Steven. "Reconstruir la ciudad: dos poemas de Gonzalo Millán y Walter Hoefler." *Literatura Chilena (creación y crítica)* 23 (1983) pp. 12-15.

GONZALO MUÑOZ

Valdés, Adriana. "Tres poetas de aquí, de ahora y un texto de Adriana Valdés." *La Separata* (Santiago) 5 (1982) pp. 4-5.

———. "Cruce de lenguajes: *Este* de Gonzalo Muñoz." *Hoy* 349 (April 1984) p. 42.

JAIME QUEZADA

Araya, Juan Gabriel. "La poesía joven chilena: Jaime Quezada (1965-1975)." *Centro de Lingüística y Literatura* (U. de Chile, Chillán) 4-5 (1977-78) pp.4-20.

Carrasco, Iván. "Poesía de Jaime Quezada: infancia y contemplación." *Nueva Revista del Pacífico* (Departamento de Literatura, Facultad de Educación y Letras, Universidad de Chile, Valparaíso) (1977) pp. 79-88.

Concha, Jaime. "Jaime Quezada: entre la infancia y las leyes." *Atenea* 421-422 (1968): pp. 490-93; rpt. *El Siglo* (Santiago) (22-VI-1969) p. 11 supl.

Hoefler, Walter. "*Astrolabio*." *El Correo de Valdivia* (14-X-1976) p.5.

Lara, Omar. "La poesía es un acto de vocación, de lucha, de rebeldía." *El Siglo* (25-II-1968) p. 16.

Pérez, Floridor. "Poesía de Jaime Quezada: una pedreada al remanso." *Las Ultimas Noticias* (Santiago) (24-X-1976) p.4.

del Solar, Hernán. "Jaime Quezada: *Astrolabio.*" *El Mercurio* (19-XII-1976) p. 5.

CLEMENTE RIEDEMANN

Bello, Marco Antonio. "*Karra Maw'n*: Versos de lluvia se ponen pantalón largo." *El Diario Austral* (Valdivia) (10-IV-1984) p. 6.

Contreras Vega, Mario. "Clemente Riedemann: Entre el poeta y el profeta." *El Diario Austral* (Valdivia) (10-X-1984) p. 2.

Rodríguez Paris, Antonieta. "Clemente Riedemann: un poeta del sur del Chile." *El Llanquihue* (Puerto Montt) (25-III-1984) p. 2

Rodríguez, Eugenio. "*Karra Maw'n* de Clemente Riedemann." *El Mercurio* (Valparaíso) (5-V-1984) p. 2.

Ulibarri, Luisa. "*Karra Maw'n.*" *Mundo* (Santiago) 18 (May, 1984) p. 66.

———. "*Karra Maw'n.*" *Pluma y Pincel* (Santiago) 14 (April-May 1984) pp. 88-89.

———. "En un poema relata la historia del sur." *24 Horas* (Valdivia) (12-III-1984) p. 8.

Aninat, Francisca. "Raúl Zurita: El paraíso y el infierno están en la propia tierra." *Que Pasa* (Santiago) 699 (30-IX-1984) pp. 44-45.

Narváez, Jorge. "Palabras de nube y nubes de palabra." *Pluma y Pincel* (Santiago) 2 (11-1-1983) p. 17.

Rojas, Waldo. "Zurita: ¿A las puertas de la esquizopoiesis?" *LAR (Revista de Literatura)* 4 & 5 (mayo de 1984) pp. 43-49.

———. "Zurita, una nueva lírica." *El Mercurio* (Santiago) (16-XII-1984) p. E3.

WALDO ROJAS

Araya, Guillermo. "*El puente oculto (poemas 1966-1980).*" *Literatura Chilena (creación y crítica)* 18 (oct.-dic., 1981).

Cantuniari, Mihai. "*Puntea ascunca.*" *Amfiteatru* 5 (May, 1981,) (Bucharest).

Castellano Girón, Hernán. "*Waldo Rojas, El puente oculto (poemas 1966-1980).*" *Trilce* 17 (1982) pp. 51-53.

———. "Waldo Rojas, *El puente oculto (poemas 1966-1980).*" *Literatura Chilena (creación y crítica)* 19 (enero/marzo, 1982) p. 34.

Concha, Jaime. "*Príncipe de naipes* de Waldo Rojas." *Atenea* 418 (1967) pp. 258-61.

Filebo. *"El puente oculto."* *Las Ultimas Noticias* (Santiago) (20-II-1983) p. 14.

Hahn, Oscar. *"El puente oculto y otros poemas."* *Handbook of Latin American Studies* 40 (University of Florida) (1978) p. 446.

Hoefler, Walter. *"Waldo Rojas, El puente oculto."* *Araucaria* 18 (1982) pp. 215-16.

Lara, Omar. *"Poesía de Waldo Rojas: el puente oculto con la realidad."* *La Nación* (Santiago) (15-X-1972) p. 12 supl.

Peri Rossi, Cristina. *"Fichas de lectura: El puente oculto,* Waldo Rojas." *Quimera* (Barcelona) 15 (enero, 1982) p. 53.

Quezada, Jaime. *"El puente de Waldo Rojas."* *Ercilla* (Santiago) (24-VI-1982) p. 51.

Schopf, Federico. *"La poesía de Waldo Rojas."* *Eco* (Colombia) 187 (1977) pp. 64-79.

ARMANDO RUBIO

Cavallo, Ascanio. *"La ciudad cuando no hay nadie."* *Hoy* 346 (7-III-1984) p. 53.

Valente, Ignacio. *"Poesía póstuma de Armando Rubio."* *El Mercurio* (6-XI-1983) p. E 3.

MANUEL SILVA ACEVEDO

Anguita, Eduardo. *"Monte de Venus."* *El Mercurio* (31-III-1982) p. E 3.

Lihn, Enrique. *"Poetas fuera o dentro de Chile 77."* *Vuelta* 15 (1978) pp. 16-22.

Quezada, Jaime. *"El oficio del bastardo."* *Ercilla* 2197 (1977).

Round. *"Dos poetas perturbados."* *Punto Final* (Santiago) 38 (1967) p. 20.

Valdés, Enrique. *"Presentación de la poesía de Manuel Silva Acevedo."* *Las Ultimas Noticias* (Santiago) (28-VIII-1977) p. 4

Valente, Ignacio. *"Manuel Silva: Lobos y ovejas."* *El Mercurio* (3-X-1976) p. III.

RAÚL ZURITA

Anguita, Eduardo. *"Zurita en su purgatorio."* *El Mercurio* (6-IV-1980) p. E2.

———. *"Reconocimiento de Zurita."* *El Mercurio* (12-XII-1982) p. E 4.

Aninat, Francisca. *"Raúl Zurita: El paraíso y el infierno están en la propia tierra."* *Que Pasa* (Santiago) 699 (30-IX-1984) pp. 44-45.

Balcells, Fernando. *"Ahora Zurita que vaciado y cortado te hace la vida."* *Bravo* (Santiago) 4, no. 1 (1980) pp. 104-105.

Brito, María Eugenia. "Conversación con Raúl Zurita." *Apsi* (Santiago) 88 (1980) pp. 22-23.

Cánovas, Rodrigo. "Lectura de *Purgatorio*: por dónde comenzar." *Hueso Húmero* (Lima) 10 (1981) pp. 170-177.

Cavallo, Ascanio. "Raúl Zurita: la poesía del dolor redimido." *Hoy* 189 (1981) pp. 41-44.

Cussen, Anthony. "El *Anteparaíso* de Zurita y la situación de la crítica en Chile." *Realidad* (Santiago) (December, 1982) pp. 21-28.

Edwards, Jorge. "Reflexiones sobre *Anteparaíso* de Raúl Zurita." *Mensaje* (Santiago) 317 (1983) pp. 140-141.

Llanos, Eduardo. "A propósito de *Anteparaíso*." *La Castaña* 2 (1983) pp. 4-6.

Martel, Juan. "Zurita: ¿infierno o paraíso?" *Huelén* 10 (1983) p. 7-15.

Narváez, Jorge. "Palabras de nube y nubes de palabra." *Pluma y Pincel* (Santiago) 2 (11-1-1983) p. 17.

O'Hara, Edgar. "Ventanas a la realidad." *La Danza del Ratón* (Buenos Aires) 3-4 (December, 1982) n.p.

Quezada, Jaime. "Zurita en su anteparaíso." *Ercilla* (November, 1982) pp. 51 & 53.

Rojas, Waldo. "Zurita: ¿A las puertas de la esquizopoiesis?" *LAR (Revista de Literatura)* 4 & 5 (mayo de 1984) pp. 43-49.

Sierra, Malú. "Raúl Zurita: el nuevo gran poeta de Chile." *Revista del Domingo (El Mercurio)* 852 (April, 1983) pp. 8-12.

Sommer, Waldemar. "Por caminos de purgatorio." *El Mercurio* (27-I-1980) p. E 5.

Valente, Ignacio. "El poeta Zurita." *El Mercurio* (7-IX-1975) p. III.

——. "Raul Zurita: *Purgatorio*." *El Mercurio* (16-XII-1979) p. E 3.

——. "Algo más sobre Zurita." *El Mercurio* (19-X-1980) p. E 3.

——. "Zurita entre los grandes." *El Mercurio* (24-X-1982) p. E 3.

——. "Zurita en la poesía chilena." *El Mercurio* (31-X-1982) p. E 3.

——. "Zurita, una nueva lírica." *El Mercurio* (Santiago) (16-XII-1984) p. E3.

Useful Studies

(General)

Bianchi, Soledad and Hernán Loyola. "Poesía chilena: la resistencia y el exilio." *Araucaria* No. 7 (1979): pp. 193-204.

——. "Jeune poésie chilienne: une generation dispersée." *Bicephale.* Europe-Amérique Latine No. 4 (Paris) Summer (1981): pp. 29-41.

——. "El movimiento artístico chileno en el conflicto actual." *Casa de las Américas* No. 130 (1982): pp. 146-154.

Bianchi, Soledad. "Un mapa por completar: la joven poesía chilena (fragmentos)." *LAR (Revista de Literatura)* 2 & 3 (abril 1983): pp. 20-21.

Bocaz, Luis. "*Trilce* 1964-1969: datos para una historia." *Trilce* (Madrid) No. 18 (1982): pp. 47-49.

——. "Reflexiones acerca de la poesía chilena contemporánea: notas para una lectura ideológica." *LAR (Revista de Literatura)* 4 & 5 (mayo 1984): pp. 34-42.

Campos, Javier. "La joven poesía chilena en el período 1961-1973." *Cuadernos Hispanoamericanos* 215 (enero 1985): pp. 128-144.

Castillo, Homero. "La literatura chilena en los Estados Unidos de América." (bibliography) *Revista Chilena de literatura* Nos. 18, 19, 20 (1981-82): pp. 159-177, 75-94, 133-145.

Cociña, Carlos. *Tendencias literarias emergentes.* Santiago: CENECA, 1983.

Coddou, Marcelo. "Poesía chilena en el exilio." *Araucaria* No. 14 (1981): pp. 99-111.

——. "Poesía chilena en el exilio a la luz de ciertos conceptos literarios fundamentales." *Hispamérica* No. 29 (1981):pp. 29-39.

Concha, Jaime. *Poesía chilena.* Santiago: Editorial Quimantú, 1973.

——. "La poesía chilena actual." *Cuadernos Americanos* No. 214 (1977): pp. 211-22.

——. "Mapa de la nueva poesía chilena." *Eco* (Colombia) No. 240 (1981): pp. 661-71.

Cornejo, Carlos and Pamela Pequeño. "Poetas jovenes: de pequeños dioses a simples mortales." *Análisis* (Santiago) No. 74 (Feb., 1984): pp. 48-49.

Dyson, John P. *La evolución de la crítica literaria en Chile.* Santiago: Editorial Universitaria, 1965.

Epple, Juan. "*Trilce* y la nueva poesía chilena." *Literatura Chilena en el Exilio* No. 9 (1979): pp. 7-10.

———. "The New Territories of Chilean Poetry." *Third Rail* (Los Angeles, CA) No. 5 (1982): pp. 2-9.

Giordano, Jaime. "Literatura y exilio." *Literatura Chilena (creación y crítica)* No. 29 (1984) pp. 5-6.

———. "Transformaciones formales en la literatura chilena después de 1973." *Areito* 9, 35 (1983): pp. 29-32.

Hoefler, Walter. "Recuento y perspectivas de la poesía chilena 1970-1976." *Cuadernos de Filología* (Antofagasta) 8 (1978):pp. 53-67.

Iturra, Carlos. "La literatura chilena en los ultimos diez años." *El Mercurio* (6-XI-1983): pp. E 4.

Jara, Alejandro. "Apuntes para un estudio de la nueva poesía chilena." *Proposiciones* (Santiago) April (1983): pp. 63-85.

Lihn, Enrique. "Sres. del primer encuentro de poesía chilena en Rotterdam." *LAR (Revista de Literatura)* 2 & 3 (abril 1983): pp. 5-9.

Maldonado, Carlos. "La Unidad Popular y el proceso cultural chileno." *Cuadernos Americanos* No. 214 (1977): pp. 177-188.

Maturana, Mariano. "El espejo sin palabras." *LAR (Revista de Literatura)* 2 & 3 (abril 1983) pp. 22-24.

Muñoz, Diego. "Encuentro Nacional de Escritores Jovenes." *Hoja x Ojo* (Santiago) No. 3 (May, 1984): n.p.

Nómez, Naín. "La poesía chilena actual: poesía vigilada y vigilante." *Primer Cuaderno de Ensayo Chileno*. Ottawa: Ediciones Cordillera, 1980, pp. 15-28.

———. "Ruptura y continuidad en la poesía chilena actual." *Literatura Chilena (creación y crítica)* 21 (1983): pp. 5-9.

O'Hara, Edgar. "Poesía chilena joven: cuerpos, signos, difuminaciones." *La palabra y la eficacia: acercamiento a la poesía joven*. Lima: Latinoamericana Editores/TAREA, 1984, pp. 107-130.

Olave, Jorge. "En Chile, el Libro ¿Libre?" *El Mercurio* (3-VII-1983): p. D 4.

Quezada, Jaime. "La palabra que nos dieron." *Las Ultimas Noticias* (Santiago) (21-X-1979): p. 4.

———. "Testimonio de un poeta chileno que vive en Chile: 1973-1983." *LAR (Revista de Literatura)* 2 & 3 (abril 1983): pp. 10-17.

Rojas, Waldo. "A 20 años de la publicación de *La pieza oscura* de Enrique Lihn: notas para una lectura generacional." Paper delivered at the Primer Coloquio Internacional de Literatura Chilena, Paris, Institut Des Hautes Etudes de L'Amérique Latine, Université Paris III-Sorbonne, 17-10 June, 1983.

———. "Los poetas de sesenta: aclaraciones en torno a una leyenda en vías de aparición." *LAR (Revista de Literatura)* 2 & 3 (abril 1983): pp. 46-55.

Rosasco, José Luis. "Poesía joven: la generación del setenta." *Atenea* (Concepción) 436 (1977) pp. 79-109.

Schopf, Federico. "Panorama del exilio." *Eco* 205 (1978): pp. 67-83.

———. "Las huellas digitales de *Trilce* y algunos vasos comunicantes." *LAR (revista de literatura)* 1 (1983): pp. 13-27.

Subercaseaux, Bernardo. "Transformaciones de la crítica literaria en Chile: 1960-1982." CENECA (Santiago) (1983).

Valente, Ignacio. "Los poetas de *Trilce*." *El Mercurio* (23-IV-1973): p.4.

———. "Poesía joven de Chile." *El Mercurio* (24-III-1974): p. 3.

Villegas, Juan. "Poesía chilena actual: censura y procedimientos poéticos." *Hispamérica* Nos. 34-35 (1983): pp. 145-154.

White, Steven. "Letter from Chile." *Third Rail* (Los Angeles, CA) No. 6 (1984): pp.30-43.

Wilson, Ricardo. "Poesía joven: entre el concepto y la desolación." *Pazquín* (Santiago) no. 1 (1979): pp. 29-30.

Zurita, Raúl. *Lenguaje, literatura y sociedad: 1973-1983*. Santiago: CENECA, 1983.

ANONYMOUS ARTICLES

"Encuentros: El 'Retiro' de los artistas, un grupo de artistas hace diagnóstico y crea organización." *Hoy* (Santiago) (21-XII-1983): p. 49.

"Escritores: un encuentro en la diversidad." *Solidaridad* (Santiago) No. 178 (1-15-VI-1984): p. 16.

Biographical Note

STEVEN F. WHITE was born in Abington, Pennsylvania in 1955 and was raised in Glencoe, Illinois. He received a B.A. in English from Williams College and an M.A. in Spanish and Hispanic American literature from the University of Oregon. His awards include the Academy of American Poets Prize in 1975 and 1977 as well as the Hubbard Hutchinson Fellowship from Williams College which enabled him to travel and to work in various Latin American countries for two years. His poems and translations have appeared in numerous magazines including *Review* (Center for Inter-American Relations), *New Directions Anthology, Nicaraguan Perspectives, Aspen Anthology, Ventana* (Managua, Nicaragua), *La Prensa Literaria* (Managua, Nicaragua), *Greenfield Review, New Orleans Review, Third Rail, Northwest Review,* and *Anthology of Magazine Verse & Yearbook of American Poetry.* In 1983, he received a Fulbright grant to translate poetry in Chile.

In addition to *Burning the Old Year,* his first volume of poetry, Mr. White has edited and translated another bilingual anthology of Latin American poetry for Unicorn Press: *Poets of Nicaragua, 1916-1979,* which was published in 1982.

JUAN ARMANDO EPPLE was born in southern Chile in 1946 and grew up in Valdivia, where he worked with the literary group Trilce. He received an Elementary School Teacher diploma from the Escuela Normal de Valdivia, and afterwards graduated as a teacher of Spanish from the Austral University of Chile. His essays on Chilean and Latin American literature have appeared in several publications, including *Cuadernos Americanos, Texto Crítico, Ideologies & Literature, RCLL, Literatura chilena (creación y crítica),* and *Araucaria.* He co-edited the anthology *Chile: poesía de la resistencia y del exilio* (1978), published simultaneously in Spain, Romania, Yugoslavia and the Soviet Union. His most recent publication is the anthology of the new Chilean short story entitled, *Cruzando la Cordillera; el cuento chileno 1973-1983* (Mexico, 1985).

He is an assistant professor of Romance Languages at the University of Oregon, and holds an M.A. and a Ph.D from Harvard University.

He is a member of the editorial board of two Chilean magazines: *Trilce* (published in Spain), and *Literatura chilena (creación y crítica)* (edited in Hollywood, California).

283